John Ashley

Origen the preacher

Being fifty short sermon notes founded upon select passages from his writings

John Ashley

Origen the preacher

Being fifty short sermon notes founded upon select passages from his writings

ISBN/EAN: 9783337113759

Printed in Europe, USA, Canada, Australia, Japan

Cover: Foto ©Lupo / pixelio.de

More available books at **www.hansebooks.com**

PATRISTIC SERMONS.

Vol. II.

ORIGEN.

NOTE TO THE READER

The paper in this volume is brittle or the inner margins are extremely narrow.

We have bound or rebound the volume utilizing the best means possible.

PLEASE HANDLE WITH CARE

GENERAL BOOKBINDING CO., CHESTERLAND, OHIO

ORIGEN THE PREACHER;

BEING

FIFTY SHORT SERMON NOTES

FOUNDED UPON

SELECT PASSAGES FROM HIS WRITINGS.

BY

JOHN M. ASHLEY, B.C.L.

VICAR OF FEWSTON.

LONDON:

J. T. HAYES, 17, HENRIETTA STREET, COVENT GARDEN;
AND LYALL PLACE, EATON SQUARE.

MDCCCLXXVIII.

ALL RIGHTS RESERVED

LONDON:
SWIFT AND CO., NEWTON STREET, HIGH HOLBORN, W.C.

CONTENTS.

	PAGE
BIOGRAPHICAL NOTICE	ix
PREFACE	xvii
INDEX OF SERMONS	xxxi
SERMONS	1

BIOGRAPHICAL NOTICE.

ORIGEN was born at Alexandria, A.D. 185. Leonidas his father, a man both of fortune and position, an ardent Christian and a lover of learning, instructed his son in the Holy Scriptures from his earliest years, causing him to commit to memory and recite some passage of Holy Writ every day. This pious seed was sown in a most kindly and fertile soil. The child was ever thinking upon that which he both read and learned, "diving into the abstruser senses of the text" (*Euseb. Eccles. Hist. lib.* vi. c. 2), and delighting the soul of a father who in word mildly rebuked, but in heart rejoiced over the thoughtful and profound reasonings of the boy. Leonidas would frequently visit the couch of his son whilst he slept, and uncovering the breast of Origen would "reverently kiss it," regarding it "as a shrine consecrated by the Divine Spirit." (*Euseb. in loco.*) In the case of

Origen "the child was truly the father of the man;" so that it was no mere figure of speech which was used by S. Jerome when writing against what he conceived to be his errors he added: "Magnus vir ab infantiâ." The fifth persecution of the Christians under Severus began A.D. 201; and in A.D. 202 Leonidas suffered martyrdom for the faith; Origen's mother having been compelled to hide her son's clothes, in order to prevent him joining his father in his death. Origen wrote to him, "Take heed not to change thy mind on account of us." His mother and six younger brothers were, by the confiscation of his father's property, left very sadly off. A rich lady of Alexandria now received Origen into her house; but he very soon earned his own bread by teaching grammar. In A.D. 203 he was appointed Professor of Grammar at the Catechetical School of Alexandria, being then eighteen years of age, and soon afterwards succeeded to the Chair of Sacred Literature. Having sold off his secular books, and leading a hard, studious, and modest life, chequered by many an act of Christian charity, gaining an ever-increasing reputation, he remained for twenty-nine years; paying occasional visits, now to Rome, then to Arabia; going to Antioch (A.D. 218) to instruct Mammæa, the mother of Alexander Severus; confuting heretics at Achaia; and receiving the gift of the Priesthood in Palestine, A.D. 228. In A.D. 231, having incurred the jealousy of Demetrius, the Bishop of Alexandria, he was degraded from the Priesthood and banished to Cæsarea; where however he was cordially welcomed by Theoctistus the bishop. From this banishment he never returned; but for twenty years after it he laboured with untiring zeal and energy in the support of that faith which was to him so precious. Illustrious men flocked to his theological school at Cæsarea from every quarter; amongst whom may be mentioned S. Gregory Thaumaturgus, afterwards Bishop of Neocæsarea. During the first four years of his residence at Cæserea Origen composed his Commentaries upon S. John and Isaiah, and commenced his Exposition of Ezekiel. The sixth, or Maximinian, persecution broke out A.D. 235, during which he wrote "An Exhortation to Martyrdom," addressed to his friends Ambrose and Theoctistus, who had been brought before the Emperor. He concealed himself first at Athens, where he finished his Commentary upon Ezekiel and continued his Commentary upon the Song of Solomon, thence he returned home, and afterwards visited Firmilian at Cæsarea in Cappadocia. In A.D. 238 Origen visited Bostra; and both convicted of and converted from his errors Beryllus, the bishop of that place. In the five years from A.D. 245-250 he preached almost daily to the people ; his sermons being taken down by transcribers, and so preserved; and at the same time he composed his eight books against Celsus; twenty-five volumes of Commentaries upon S. Matthew, and a like number of volumes upon the Minor Prophets; a letter to Philip the Emperor, and one to Severa his wife. The seventh, or Decian, persecution, A.D. 250, raged with great severity at Cæsarea. Bishops Alexander and Babylas both died in prison. Origen was for several days confined in the deepest recesses of a dungeon; laden with an iron collar; stretched on the rack; threatened with fire ; subject to torments just moderated sufficiently to save his life. His prison Epistles, composed during his confinement, are unfortunately lost. At the time of his liberation Origen was sixty-six years old; worn out and broken in heart and body he lingered on for three years more, and died at Tyre, in the second year of the reign of Gallus, A.D. 253, at the age of sixty-nine. Truly he was of the number of those saints of whom "the world was not worthy." Origen was a most noble champion for the truth, hence his surname of Adamantius; so called either from the strength of his reasoning (Photius), or from his hardness in resisting error. (S. Jerome.) He was the most learned man of his day; he was very holy in his life and conversation; and his influence for good was widely felt over the whole length and breadth of the Catholic Church; and yet that Church proved a most ungrateful mother to so worthy a son; just as the world, by its bitter persecution, showed its hatred to the valiant Christian scholar and priest. Origen suffered alike from the Church and from the world; from the fold within as well as from the wolves without. Besides this twofold persecution, another remarkable fact in his history is, that whilst he was so deep an explorer and so ardent an admirer of the mystical sense of Holy Scripture, he was most literal in the application of its simplest precepts to his own life, even to the extent of fulfilling in his own person the hint given in S. Matt. xix. 12. Again, we note the most imperfect and unsatisfactory state in which his writings have come down to us. Origen wrote six thousand tracts, or volumes as they were then called; most of which are lost; and of the few preserved to us the larger portion exist only in the Latin version of Rufinus, who tampered so considerably with the original, that it is difficult to determine what was composed by the author, and what by the translator. Yet of priceless value, even in their present imperfect state, are these memorials which time has spared to us of this great theologian and Biblical critic. Profound scholarship; deep religious feeling; unwearied industry; a large, loving heart; a genius that shed its bright rays of glory over his every page; a long life of earnest, hard, self-denial, consecrated entirely to the service of his Divine Master; a nature noble alike in head and heart; it is sad and sickening to think of such a one as this—the possessor of all these varied gifts—honoured and respected even by those who were most jealous of his fame—wearied even to death by the tortures and barbarities of the Cæsarean prison—dragging his poor old broken, mangled body from the prison and the torture chamber, to find a grave in Tyre, like as the wounded stag betakes himself to the waters. The heathen may have pointed the finger of scorn at the bent body and bowed head as Origen, the old man, passed along the highways of Tyre, but from them one day will the confession be wrung: "We fools counted his end to be without honour; now is He numbered among the children of God, and his lot is among the saints."

PREFACE.

THE present series of Sermon Notes have been founded upon such remarks and expositions of Origen as most arrested the writer's attention when reading over his works with an eye to such a use of them. He does not say that either Origen's most striking speculations, or his most startling examples of mysticism, will find any representation in the following pages. As with his past use of S. Augustine, so with his present use of Origen; and he trusts, also, that with his future use of S. Ambrose, whose writings will next be treated in a similar manner; his aim and object is to present such germs of thought as might be most usefully and practically worked up into instructions fit to form the basis of sermons suitable to be delivered from our parish pulpits. In parochial preaching, the less of speculative and of philosophical truth that there is the better; and the simpler it is the more useful will be its service. That which is really required in such preaching is, that the great truths of the Faith—that its old leading principles, axioms, and foundations—be ever presented, as far as possible, in new forms, and be pressed home to men's hearts and consciences in the most clear and striking manner possible. Hence this little book is not to be considered, any more than its companion, " S. Augustine the Preacher," as containing any fair representation of either the works or the teaching of this great master of the Alexandrian School, but simply as turning some small portion of his writings to a practical account. Of course the general tone of religious teaching in the second century must differ considerably from that of the nineteenth. Sixteen hundred years of prayer and thought must have made their abiding and expanding influence felt by the whole body of the Church of Jesus Christ; hence the present subjective nature of our religious teaching as compared with the almost purely objective form which is presented to us in the writings of the Ante-Nicene Fathers. We admit of an appeal to them, as authoritative exponents of Christian dogma; but surely we have passed beyond them in our applications of that dogma to men's hopes, fears, sins, struggles, and victories over temptation and error. Yet the works of the great Fathers of the Church, taking the most liberal and unecclesiastical view of the matter, are indeed vast store-houses of theological wealth; full of thoughts holy and impressive, and which have all the charms of novelty for those who take in hand their serious and minute study for the first time. It is not too much to state, that if any really good and telling modern sermon were analysed, many, if not all, of its best things would be found to be embodied in the writings of one or more of the Fathers, and expressed, it may be, by them in better, clearer, and terser language than that which is used by the modern preacher. In the selection of the passages from Origen, which have been expanded in the present little book, the same principles have been applied as in the case of S. Augustine; but the task in this latter case has proved to be a somewhat easier one, because the works of Origen which have come down to us, the treatise "Against Celsus;" the "Peri Archon;" the several fragments of his "Hexapla" (a magnificent edition of which, most ably edited by Mr. Field, has recently been completed and issued from the

Clarendon Press), and a few other minor pieces alone excepted, are for the most part hortatory; his commentaries even upon Isaiah, Jeremiah, Ezekiel, Psalms, Canticles, and especially those upon the earlier Historic Books of the Old Testament, are all put together in the form of homilies, and they partake most strongly of a homeletic character. The very simplicity of the style of Origen, of which the extant Greek text of some of his writings affords abundant proof, must have rendered him a most acceptable preacher in his own day; and forms no inapt vehicle for the still useful translation of his thoughts to our own times, after the lapse of more than sixteen centuries. The homilies upon SS. Matthew and John, and the Prophet Jeremiah, are alone fully represented in their original Greek form; the invaluable exposition upon the other books of the Old Testament, save a small part of the commentaries upon Genesis, Exodus, Joshua, and the Psalms, exist only in the Latin translation of Ruffinus, Jerome, and other unknown translators. Yet this fact, whilst it often suggests a doubt as to what Origen did or did not really write, cannot wholly take away the charm which those homilies possess even in their present mangled and foreign garb. For Origen was a very sweet writer; so earnest, thoughtful, and brilliant; he had such a deep and loving knowledge of Holy Scripture; he compared so very forcibly things new with things old; that in the reading of His writings no one could be made to feel that they were sitting down as a duty to pore over the pages of a great Father of the Church, with a somewhat heavy task before them, but that they were rather gathering up the thoughts of a most interesting and original thinker, and filling their commonplace-book, as they went on with a great diversity of new and striking thoughts, hints, interpretations, comparisons, and other kinds of sermon lore. It is true that Origen was a bold speculator; a deep mysticist; a whilelom 1... mist; a fair representative of the activity and brilliancy of thought which was in general the characteristic of the Alexandrian School in its best and palmiest days. Ye for all this, he is a most gentle, loving, and persuasive writer, and one that carries his reader so completely with him, that he allows him to be overcome with no sense either of weariness or of irksomeness. And no wonder that this should be so, seeing that the homilies of Origen are not dry dogmatic commentaries upon the Inspired Text, but they are a series of what may be truly called panoramas of Holy Scripture, in which history, doctrine, moral and spiritual applications all pass in an infinite variety before the eye of the reader. Things new and old are so originally and yet judiciously blended together, that the unity of Holy Scripture comes home to the student of Origen as a great reality. Whether or not also the reader may be willing to accept the several allegorical and mystical senses of the Sacred Text which are propounded by Origen, they are, as a rule, so original and striking, supported by such abundant proof, commended by such a fulness of illustration, that they cannot fail to arrest the attention; even when they do not command the assent of the understanding; they set the mind a thinking, and remove every trace of dulness from his page. The great problems of life; the nature of the soul and its attributes; its states after death; its relation to the kingdoms of light and of darkness; to the mysteries of being and to the scheme of grace, are subjects upon which Origen is ever ready to treat; for his theology consists not so much in a system of belief, as in the application of Revelation to unfold many of the mysteries by which man and his destiny are surrounded. The teaching of Origen is not dead but living; it deals not with abstract truths but with living verities, which are ever able to exert a quickening influence upon the living, loving, fearing souls of men. The strange vitality of the old Greek life seems to have transfused itself into his words and works. Origen is essentially a Father of Eastern rather than of Western Christendom.

If it be permitted to recall the general impressions which the study of Origen's writings have left with the author, first and foremost stands out in his every page, nay, every thought, the figure of our Lord Jesus Christ. He is never absent from his mind and affections: every incident, record, doctrine, or history is referred to Him, as being a type, prophecy, or adumbration of His Blessed Person or Work. Jesus Christ is the sun of Origen's system of theology, around which the Church, the Scriptures, and the Saints revolve in their appointed courses, like the moon and stars. We see Him everywhere—"all Genesis through"—as giving the true significance to every historical record of Old Testament History; as unfolding in Himself the deeper meaning of the Psalms; as alone being the true key to the interpretation of the Song of Solomon; as imparting a solemn prophetic utterance to the words of Isaiah, Jeremiah, Ezekiel, and the other Prophets; shining in His more perfect splendour in His deeds and sayings in the Gospels. And Origen also takes us into the higher life of Jesus Christ as being the Son of God, by means of which life " He was truly substantially [substantialiter] ever present in Moses and in the Prophets " (Geneb. ii. 83, A); and having been made an High Priest for ever after the order of Melchizedec (Ps. cx. 4), " was able by the dispensation of His death to divide the veil of the Temple ' in twain, from the top to the bottom,' so that the things within could be seen by eyes which were able to see." (Geneb. ii. 130, L.) In fact, the several offices, types, names, and titles of our Blessed Lord are so fully treated of by Origen, that it would be quite possible to weave out of his works a profound and spiritual "Life of Christ;" one that would fathom, as far as the human mind can do so, the deep mysteries of His twofold being and nature. Origen takes a very exalted view of personal holiness. " They are said to be holy who have consecrated themselves to God" (Geneb. i. 166, M.), fulfilling (S. Matt. xvi. 24; Gal. ii. 20). The saints are clouds (Geneb. i. 371, C), into which God's truth reaches (Ps. lvii. 10), who are to withhold their rain when souls are found to be unworthy of the heavenly shower. (Isa. v. 6.) They are also the hills, upon which, as at the Mount of Transfiguration, the Lord showed His glory. (Geneb. i. 341, B.) They are also God's tabernacles of witness; (Geneb. i. 119, D.) are reckoned as being the possessors of true being (Geneb. ii. 173, G), and as being the lights of the world. (Geneb. ii. 171, A.) Full of thoughts like these is every page of Origen's writing; yet we must be content with a bare mention, in conclusion, of the means by which a knowledge of his works can best be gained.

With respect to the editions of the works of Origen. The "*Editio Princeps*" is that of the Benedictines of S. Maur, which is comprised in four folio volumes. This great work was commenced by Charles de la Rue, a pupil of Montfaucon, with the assistance of his nephew Charles Vincent de la Rue, who completed the work after his uncle's death, and published the fourth and last volume at Paris in 1759. Without the Commentary, it was republished by Oberthür, at Würtzbourg, in fifteen octavo volumes. It has also been reprinted by Migne. Next in value to this sumptuous

Benedictine Edition, is the Greek text of the Commentaries of Origen upon Holy Scripture, by the learned Peter Daniel Huet, Bishop of Avranches, accompanied by a Latin translation, which was the work of various hands : Huet himself translating the "Commentary upon S. Matthew;" Ambrose Ferrar, that upon S. John, which is the longest and most perfect of Origen's exegetical works; Francis Viger, the fragments of the Pentateuch; Valesius and Petavius, the Psalms; S. Jerome, the Homilies on Jeremiah. Huet's Origen is in two volumes folio. An elaborate treatise upon Origen and his writings, entitled "*Origeniana*," consisting of 278 closely printed folio pages of Latin, is prefixed to this edition, which was published by John Berthelin, at Rheims, A.D. 1668. Merlinus first, and afterwards Erasmus, published all the Latin remains of Origen in two folio volumes, both at Paris and Basle. He was followed by Gilbert Genebrard, Regius Professor of Hebrew in the University of Paris, who made a larger collection of the writings of Origen, and published his collection at Paris, in the years 1574, 1604, 1619, and also at Basle in 1620. It is to Genebrard's first Paris edition of 1574 that most of the references in the following pages refer. It is a very complete edition of the works of Origen, and being easy of possession, both as to its price and the number of copies of it in the market, it was deemed the most useful one to which reference could be made in the present book; an exception being made in some few instances in favour of Huet's edition of 1668. "The Commentary upon St. Matthew" in Genebrard's edition is from the pen of Erasmus. A very convenient and accurate edition of the "Contra Celsum" was published at Cambridge, in quarto, in 1677, by William Spencer, a Fellow of Trinity College. It consists of the Greek text, accompanied by the Latin translation by Sigismund Gelen, which appears also in Genebrard's edition published just a century before it. "The Dialogue against Marcion," edited in quarto, with Greek and English, by John Rodolph Wetstein, appeared at Basil, 1674. This is the edition which is referred to in the Sermon Notes. There can be no doubt, from internal testimony, that this Dialogue belongs to a later age than that of Origen; but as the quotations taken from it are strictly Origenistic in thought, and as it always forms part of his works, it has been twice quoted on the present occasion. No use has been made of William Reading's beautiful edition of Origen's treatise "On Prayer," which Tonson and Watts published at London, A.D. 1728.

The student who is desirous of thoroughly mastering the writings of Origen, should consult the treatise upon his life, writings, and opinions, which forms the ninth and the greater part of the tenth volumes of Gottfrid Lumper's "Historia Theologico Critica Sanctorum Patrum," which was published at Ausburg, A.D. 1792, 1793. It contains the pith and marrow of Huet's "Origeniana," also of Bernard Marechal's "Concordantia Patrum" (2 vols. fol. Ausburg, 1763), and of the notes, dissertations, etc., of the Benedictine edition. Lumper often transcribes not only the quotations from Origen, which are given by Marechal, but actually his comments upon them, word for word. It is a curious fact that both the "Historia" and the "Concordantia" were published by Rieger, the former just thirty years after the latter. The treatise of Lumper consists of nine sections and one supplement. These nine sections are divided into "chapters," which are in turn subdivided into "articles." The first "section" embraces the life of Origen; the second, his writings; the third, his doctrine; the fourth contains observations, disciplinal and historical; the fifth, observations philosophical, hermeneutical and exegetical; the sixth, observations historico-critical; the seventh, observations philosophico-theological; the eighth, the opinions of certain learned men concerning Origen; the ninth, and last section, gives a *resumé* of the whole treatise, and a catalogue of the several editions of the works of Origen. The fifth section is perhaps the most interesting portion of Lumper's exhaustive and elaborate disquisition: it gives a synopsis of Origen's method of interpreting Holy Scripture, and in a series of well illustrated "articles" discusses, amongst other points, the threefold sense of Scripture; the value of the literal sense; the seeming imperfections of Scripture; the support which the New Testament itself lends to the system of mystical interpretation; certain rules for the determination of the mystical sense; and lastly it explains very completely the system of Scriptural interpretation which is generally adopted by Origen. The valuable amount of exegetical matter which Lumper has contrived to amass in the short space of thirty-one pages is truly, marvellous. The thorough digestion of this one "section" would afford any student valuable material upon which to occupy his reading for a considerable period. Anyway Lumper's treatise is the best companion with which we are acquainted to the text of this truly great Father.

Although in the following pages there is necessarily more of the present writer than there is of Origen, it is trusted that these short Sermon Notes will not be found to be unacceptable to many who have neither the time nor the opportunity to read him for themselves; that some of the seeds of thought which they contain may germinate and take root in other more fruitful and more gifted minds, and may so become the humble means of bringing the mysteries of God's Kingdom and grace home with a new force and power to many souls; and that they may above all things tend to the honour and glory of our Lord Jesus Christ and His Holy Church; to Whom be glory, praise, and dominion for ever and ever.

The third volume of the present series will be founded upon S. Ambrose.   J. M. A.

Laus Deo.

INDEX OF SERMONS.

	PAGE

SERMON I.
JESUS LIVING (Easter Day).—*Gal.* ii. 20 1

SERMON II.
THE CHILDREN OF THE SOUL.—*Dan.* iv. 19 5

SERMON III.
SORROW.—*S. Matt.* vi. 20 10

SERMON IV.
GOD'S IMAGE.—*Gen.* i. 27 16

SERMON V.
THE LAW OF SYMPATHY.—*S. Matt.* xiii. 58 20

SERMON VI.
THE STRONG MAN OF DOUBT.—*S. Matt.* xii. 29 26

SERMON VII.

IMPRESSIONS.—*S. Matt.* xii. 35 31

SERMON VIII.

THE ETERNAL RECORD.—*Jer.* x. 19 36

SERMON IX.

THE GARDENER.—*S. John* xx. 15 41

SERMON X.

THE MIDDLE WAY.—*S. John* xiv. 6 46

SERMON XI.

THE RIGHT HEART.—*Acts* viii. 21 51

SERMON XII.

HEAVEN OUR PERFECTION.—*Ps.* l. 2 57

SERMON XIII.

PERFECT FAITH.—*S. John* ii. 23, 24 60

SERMON XIV.

THE SWORD OF TEACHING.—*S. Matt.* x. 34 65

SERMON XV.

GUILTY WORDS.—*S. Matt.* xii. 37 69

	PAGE
SERMON XVI.	
THE ESTATE OF MAN.—*Ps.* viii. 5	73
SERMON XVII.	
FELLOW-WORKERS WITH GOD.—2 *Cor.* vi. 1	78
SERMON XVIII.	
THE TABERNACLES OF KNOWLEDGE.—*Num.* xxiv. 5	83
SERMON XIX.	
STUMBLINGBLOCKS.—*S. Matt.* xviii. 7	88
SERMON XX.	
THE ALTAR OF THE HEART.—*Heb.* xiii. 10	93
SERMON XXI.	
HELL.—*Isa.* l. 11	98
SERMON XXII.	
HOLY PERSUASION.—2 *Cor.* v. 11	102
SERMON XXIII.	
THE MYSTERY OF PROBATION.—*Deut.* xiii. 3	107
SERMON XXIV.	
THE LIGHT OF TRUTH.—2 *S. Pet.* i. 19	112

SERMON XXV.
A Holy Man.—*Levit.* xxi. 7 117

SERMON XXVI.
The Wine of Joy.—*S. Matt.* xxvi. 29 .. 122

SERMON XXVII.
The Knowledge of Jesus.—*S. Matt.* xxv. 31, 32 127

SERMON XXVIII.
Immortality.—*S. John* xvii. 3 132

SERMON XXIX.
The Spiritual Image.—*S. Matt.* xxii. 20 138

SERMON XXX.
Attempts.—*Exod.* xiv. 12 142

SERMON XXXI.
The Hallowing Presence.—*Joshua* v. 15 146

SERMON XXXII.
The Noble Ruin.—*S. Matt.* xxiv. 1 151

SERMON XXXIII.
Spiritual Vision.—*S. Luke* xvi. 23 156

Index of Sermons.

SERMON XXXIV.
HOLY DISCIPLINE.—*S. Matt.* xviii. 8, 9 161

SERMON XXXV.
THE GRAND RECEIPT.—*S. Matt.* xv. 11 166

SERMON XXXVI.
CHRISTIAN CULTURE.—*S. Matt.* xv. 13 171

SERMON XXXVII.
THE MORAL PRESENCE.—*Gal.* ii. 20 176

SERMON XXXVIII.
THE HOUSE OF JESUS.—*S. Matt.* xiii. 36 .. 181

SERMON XXXIX.
THE CONSENT TO SIN.—*Eph.* iv. 27 187

SERMON XL.
THE CARE OF JESUS.—*S. Luke* x. 33 192

SERMON XLI.
THE GOOD BEHIND.—1 *Cor.* ii. 8 199

SERMON XLII.
THE DESCENT FROM THE MOUNTAIN.—*S. Matt.* viii. 1   205

Index of Sermons.

PAGE

SERMON XLIII.
JESUS THE SUN.—*Mal.* iv. 2 211

SERMON XLIV.
DEATH UNTO LIFE.—2 *Cor.* iv. 12 .. 217

SERMON XLV.
THE INWARD EYE.—2 *Cor.* ii. 16 223

SERMON XLVI.
THE SHADOW OF LIFE.—*S. Matt.* xix. 17 229

SERMON XLVII.
THE WORDS OF JESUS CHRIST.—*S. John* vii. 46 235

SERMON XLVIII.
CONSCIENCE.—*Rom.* ii. 15 240

SERMON XLIX.
THE ONE GOSPEL.—*S. Mark* xvi. 15 246

SERMON L.
NIGHT.—*S. John* xiii. 30 252

SERMON I.
JESUS LIVING.
(*Easter Day.*)

"Christ liveth in me."—*Gal.* ii. 20.

Origen.—"In some Jesus lives, in others, indeed, He has died. Jesus lives in Paul, and in Peter, and in all those who can truly say, 'I live; yet not I, but Christ liveth in me.' (Gal. ii. 20.) Again he says, 'To me to live is Christ, and to die is gain.' (Phil. i. 21.) In such as these, therefore, Jesus is deservedly said to live. But in whom has Jesus died? In those, without doubt, who by often repenting and often falling away are said to mock at the death of Jesus. Do you yourself consider with yourself. If when you are thinking of covetousness and desiring the goods of another, can you say, 'Christ liveth in me?' Or if when inflamed with anger, heated with jealousy, or stimulated by envy, or raging with passion, or swelling with pride, or attacking with cruelty, can you in all these things say that 'Christ liveth in me?' So.

therefore, Christ is dead in sinners, in whom is neither righteousness, patience, and truth, and not any of those things which Christ works."—*In Jud. Hom.* ii. *Geneb.* vol. i. p. 211, A.

What is that life which Jesus lives in the souls of the faithful? It is a life which is—

I. *Quickening.*—Many a soul seems to be either asleep or dead; barely giving any signs of life or animation; capable of small emotion; sluggish in affection; wanting in any high aspiration. A chord is touched; that soul is quickened into life; the dormant element of love, or hope, or resolution is kindled into action and development. When the soul receives the Presence of Jesus by Sacramental union, by faith and prayer, then Jesus is living within it; then all things are made new to it. " The love of God constraineth " it. It awakes, as it never has awakened before, to a new sense of its own sin; of the Lord's redeeming love; of the deadly nature of its former estate. " It was dead and is alive again." This quickening life—1) intensifies every feeling; 2) raises within the soul a new life; 3) is the parent of new desires and resolutions. It makes a true and real Easter in the soul.

II. *Productive.*—All life is more or less productive; only death is barren and unfruitful. Jesus living in the soul, it produces its true and proper fruits. He cannot be there without working His works of life. Such are—1) Repentance; a turning away from past sins; sins which were suited to the old condition of being, but which are utterly unsuited to the new. As we adapt ourselves to our several stations in life, so he in whom Jesus lives, adapts himself to the Life of Jesus Christ. 2) Holiness; the cultivation of all the Christian graces; so that the soul may become like Him through Whom it now lives. It is a putting off " of the old man and a putting on of the new." This new man is immortal; so when Jesus lives in the soul He makes a true Easter therein.

III. *Undying.*—The life on earth is essentially a dying life; dying, inasmuch as it so very soon passes away; dying, since the present is ever dying to the past; dying as relating to things which in themselves are mortal. When Jesus lives in the soul, His life-giving Presence—1) never passes away; it remains there through death; it waxes stronger when the soul is freed from the bondage of corruption; it attains to its full strength in the Resurrection state. 2) Allows of no conditions of time: "Behold, I am alive for evermore;" it is the ever-present power of an endless life. 3) It is concerned with things, beings, and states of being which are as deathless as itself. Therefore is this undying life, flowing from an undying Presence, the cause of an eternal Easter in the soul.

IV. *Sanctifying.*—In some persons there is a certain grace and dignity of manner and speech which gives a charm to their very presence ; to their words, be they ever so simple ; to their actions, be they ever so common. When Jesus lives in the soul He gives this charm to our lowly life ; He invests our thoughts, words, and deeds, with the—1) good which flows from His own holiness ; 2) true, which reflects His own perfect truth ; 3) beautiful, which shadows forth the indwelling Presence of one Who is "fairer than the children of men." So to gild and to glorify man's common daily life cannot but be an hallowing Easter to the soul.

Epilogue.—O Christian soul ! if thou hast fallen into a second death of trespasses and sins, rest not day nor night until He Who now stands and knocks at the door of thy heart (Rev. iii. 20) may find an entrance there ; then will begin thy true Easter ; then " risen with Christ " thou wilt truly live ; since Jesus lives in thee in time and in eternity.

SERMON II.

THE CHILDREN OF THE SOUL.

"His thoughts troubled him."—*Dan.* iv. 19.

Origen.—" There is therefore no period when the soul does not bring forth. The soul ever brings forth, ever generates children. But that generation is blessed indeed which is produced, having been conceived by the Word of God; and this is the generation of children through which it will become saved."— *In Numb.*, *Hom.* xx., *Geneb.* vol. i. p. 157, A.

"The thoughts which proceed from our heart—either the memory of certain actions, or the contemplation of certain matters and causes—we find to proceed sometimes from our very selves, at other times they are accustomed to be formed from our contrary powers." —*Peri Archon.*, *lib.* iii. c. 2, *Geneb.* vol. i. p. 458, K.

This reproductive power of the soul forms its greatest prerogative and responsibility. "Out of the heart" proceed thoughts high, holy, heavenly, and low, "earthly, sensual, devilish." Hence the solemn charge, "Keep thy heart with all diligence" (Prov. iv. 23), and the prayer, "O God, try me, and know my thoughts." (Ps. cxxxix. 23.) The due and proper discipline of the soul is one of the most important and hardest portions of the Christian life. We cry shame upon those who neglect the children of their bodies, leaving them ill-cared for, and not properly provided with the necessaries of life. But what care do we bestow in order to rightly control, discipline, and arrange our thoughts, "the children of the soul?" Yet these latter are worthy of all culture, as being—

I. *Numberless.*—What hundreds, thousands, nay, tens of thousands of thoughts pass over the mind in the course of one day. Some originating in the soul itself, others borrowed from those with whom we converse, being indirectly or partially formed from our external life and conversation; these, "brethren, which have at the same time worthily sprung in the souls of others" (*Plato Phædr.* 278, B), which we have adopted and assimilated with our own. Multiply these numbers by the days of a week, of a month, of a year, by periods of twenty, forty, sixty, or eighty years. During the waking hours of the longest life "there is no period when the soul does not bring forth" her children, more or less strong, wholly or more partially formed. These numberless creations of the soul should lead to a sense of fear and shame, founded upon the reflection that out of so vast a sum there must be—1) many which are sinful; 2) more which are valueless and unprofitable; 3) few, very few, it may be, which are worthy of our received grace, of our knowledge, and of our powers of mind. How large is the portion of dross intermingled with the smallest and fewest grains of the pure metal which will stand the trying fire. (1 Cor. iii. 13.) Very worthless are many of the "children of the soul."

II. *Changeless.*—A thought once issued from the soul is changeless. It may be succeeded by other thoughts, and so driven out of the mind; it may be repented of and atoned for; but when once formed, it has passed beyond the recall or power of the mind to alter it. The tone and complexion of the thought depends wholly upon its first formation. Material things can be refashioned and rearranged. Groups of thought and knowledge can be varied in the several expressions of them; but the primary thought remains entire and perfect, as it existed at the first moment of its formation. This consideration should induce both care and prayer that the "children of the soul" themselves may be pure and holy; which can only be the case when the habit and disposition of the soul itself is—1) Purified by divine grace;

2) Chastened by divine discipline; 3) Watered by Divine love. When the soil is good, the produce is good; and good fruit is the produce of a good tree. (S. Matt. vii. 17.)

III. *Immortal.*—A child of the soul; a thought once born, being changeless, can never die. It may be put away, be forgotten, be hidden behind the million other creations of the brain, yet it exists still. It is recorded by God; it lives for ever. One thought rapidly displaces another, or else the soul would stagnate under the accumulation of its own productions. We should be filled with horror and awe could the thoughts of one short year be placed before the mind in a moment of time. How many hopes, desires, fears, and expectations have chased away each other during this short interval? Are these "children of the soul," this vast multitude, really mine? 1) Mine by production, the produce of my brain? 2) Mine by possession, belonging to myself and none other? 3) Mine, to be owned by me one day before the judgment-seat of God?

IV. *Secret and spiritual.*—These "children of the soul" are known only to God and the soul itself. Hence the evil thought lacks the restraints of earthly shame, such as pride and the like. Whilst word and deed are kept strictly under control, thought is allowed to run riot without let or hindrance. Hence the prayer (Ps. xix. 12) against "secret faults;" evil "children of the soul," which are not subject to the ordinary laws of life. These secret and spiritual children, unless subject to an unceasing watchfulness, become—1) overbearing and dominant; 2) ugly in form; 3) morbid in substance. They become "a law unto themselves" in the worst sense, and that law is but the expression of our corrupt and fallen nature.

V. *Influential.*—These "children of the soul" are all powerful in—1) this life: they make or mar our happiness, for the mind is truly the the mirror of life. 2) The life to come: they will save us or condemn us, as they witness for or against us, as being holy or sinful children in the sight of the Almighty Judge.

Epilogue.—Consider then, O Christian soul, that thy thoughts, the children of thy mind, are thy very own; thy voluntary offspring, which thou alone canst transmit to others: and ever pray to be preserved from producing children of perdition.

SERMON III.
SORROW.

"Lay up for yourselves treasures in heaven, where neither moth nor rust doth corrupt."— *S. Matt.* vi. 20.

Origen.—" It can be rightly said of him who has laid up treasure in heaven, that not one moth of the affections can touch his spiritual and heavenly riches. I have said moth of the affections, taking occasion from Proverbs, in which is written, " As a worm in wood, so sorrow consumeth the heart of a man " (Prov. xxv. 20, LXX.), for sorrow is the worm and moth consuming the heart which hath not its treasure in spiritual and heavenly things, in which, if any one layeth up treasure, he will have his heart in heaven, since ' Where your treasure is, there will your heart be also.'—(S. Matt. vi. 21.)" *Comment. S. Matt.* *Huet.* vol. i. p. 220, A.

Truly can that " sorrow of the world," which " worketh death " (Rom. vii. 10), be called the " moth of the affections." " The affections " represent the desires, yearnings, and aspirations of life, as well as those sacred and holy ties by which, in this world, hearts are knit and bound the one to the other. The moth " corrupts " by slowly consuming; eats into and away the substance; leaving sometimes a form which a breath of air resolves into the finest dust—a form, which for the moment takes the semblance of the real object itself. Sorrow, like the moth, consumes slowly the substance, the reality and joy of life, leaving but a passionless feeble image of its former self in its stead; the sorrow which flows from a life disappointment, unhealed by submission; from a sin cherished in secret, and not cast out of the soul by repentance; from a sore bereavement under which the merciful chastisement of a Heavenly Father is unrecognized. Unholy sorrow is a very moth, silently, slowly, surely, day by day, preying upon the body of its victim, and only ceasing in its dire work when nothing further remains to corrupt. Ungodly sorrow —" the sorrow of the world "—eats out of life its—

I. *Glory and beauty.*—The face of nature is most beautiful in spring-tide, when coldness, darkness, " snow and vapour, wind and storm," give place to the gentle zephyr, the genial sunshine, the clear blue æther, and every living organism is nascent with life, developing on all sides new and tender forms of living beauty. The moth of winter has been slain by the Spirit of Spring. So is the young life whilst in its spring-tide; whilst its soul hath been as yet undimmed by sorrow, new thoughts, feelings, and faculties, develope in it from day to day; there is a glory and beauty in it—a bloom of life upon it—which vanishes under the first rude touch of the stern hand of sorrow. Man's present life—destined to remain for so short a time sorrowless, and in its first beauty—is a type and emblem of what our own eternal life shall be in that sinless state in which tears shall be wiped from every eye, and the days of our mourning shall be for ever ended. This "moth of the affections"—1) corrodes the fair surface of life; 2) darkens the joys of earth; 3) overshadows the trust of the soul in the providence and in the mercy of God.

II. *Desires and Aspirations.*—No plant can grow with a canker at its root. No soul can put forth its aspirations and desires when sorrow, the "moth of the affections," is poisoning the current of life. Sorrow, like sin, stays the growth of the soul in all that is noblest and most blessed, even as some forms of disease stay the growth of the body, and restrain the manhood within the limits of childhood. The soul, when it is free and unfettered, is ever rising, carried before the winds of love, faith, and knowledge, towards a higher and still a higher point of attainment. Sorrow passes over the soul, and—1) Dries it up, even as the sirocco does the delicate flower, nipping its bud, staying its development. 2) Weighs and presses it down; so that all its energy is constrained, and at length perishes from the want of use and exercise. What is called a blighting influence, is often nothing more than a weight of sorrow, carried in secret and borne in silence; a burden that is gradually and continuously pressing all the higher life out of the soul. 3) Blunts its finer feelings and sensibilities, until it loses its keen sense and appreciation of that which once awakened in it the loftiest emotions, or excited it to the highest degree of enthusiasm.

III. *Strength.*—How strong is the frame of those who have never been laid low by sickness, and who still rejoice in a vigorous and unimpaired manhood. Such are in the fulness of their strength. When disease has once passed over them in a malignant form, they may recover their health, but they are never again as they once were; their strength and immunity from pain has gone from them. So is it when sorrow —the " moth of the affections "—rests upon the soul. It weakens it, and deprives it of the threefold strength of—1) Purpose; it now no longer, as it used to do, holds on its own way with a tenacity of purpose that neither opposition can daunt, nor obstacle hinder. Shaken by sorrow, the soul becomes weak in fully acting up to the former behests of its will. 2) Endeavour; it strives not as heretofore, when supported by the mighty power of an unchecked life. Faltering and wayward are the efforts which it now makes to rise above and superior to the circumstances of life. 3) Endurance ; its toughness is turned to brittleness, and it now sinks down into an apathetic state, without that power of patient waiting which, sooner or later, must bring victory in its train.

IV. *Substance.*—The moth eats away the substance upon that which it feeds; so does the "moth of the affections"—sorrow—eat away by degrees the substance of the soul. Consuming—1) its powers ; 2) Destroying its hopes. 3) Loosening all its hold upon that which, for its great profit, it had once made its own. After sorrow has fulfilled its "perfect work, but the semblance, shadow, or image, rather than the substance of the soul itself, is left. Want of heartiness is want of that substance which the "moth of the affections" has by slow stages eaten away.

Epilogue.—Lay up then your heart and your treasure in heaven, where moth doth not corrupt; remembering, that "not one moth of the affections" can touch heavenly and spiritual riches. Let holy sorrow for sin be ever cherished ; sacred sorrow for loved ones departed, not wholly be denied ; a deep sorrow for the sufferings of others maintain a kindly sympathy in the soul ; but that morbid sorrow of the world ; that regret over defeated ambition, lost honours, departed wealth; never let place be given to it for a moment. Cast it from you as if it were a viper. Ere it gain a firm footing in the inward man, kill it by—1) Prayer; which will exorcise it as if it were an evil spirit. 2) An earnest effort of the will, giving it not a moment's peace. 3) Using all the circumstances of life against it. An old Greek bard once sang words which may thus be roughly rendered into our mother tongue:

> " Oh cast from life for ever sorrow's bane,
>   Kinsman to life although it be,
> And griefless mortal life is hard to gain.
> Grief brings disease to man his direst harm,
>   The fortunate are sorrow free.
> Such peace, the vessel's port, life's harbour calm."
>   —*Poet. Min.* p. 527.

Language this which is capable of translation into a higher meaning if we read "the holy" for "the fortunate;" since the former carry with them that Blessed Presence, even of Him Who promised once, "your sorrow shall be turned into joy" (S. John xiv. 20); and Who bade the faithful be comforted by the words, "In the world ye shall have tribulation: but be of good cheer; I have overcome the world."

SERMON IV.
GOD'S IMAGE.

"God created man in His own image."—*Gen.* i. 27.

Origen.—"Man was made in the image of God, in whom also the marks of the Divine image are manifestly known; not by the likeness of the body, which is polluted, but through the prudence, justice, moderation, virtue, wisdom, and discipline of the mind; and lastly, by all the choir of graces which are present with God by substance [per substantiam], and can be present in man by industry [per industriam], and by the imitation of God, as also the Lord signified in the Gospel, saying, "Be ye therefore perfect," etc. (S. Matt. v. 48.)—*De Princip. lib.* iv. *Geneb.* vol. i. p. 476, G.

We do not know, neither can we understand, what God is really like. The reflexion of His attributes which we see in the created universe, physical and moral, alone affords to our imperfect minds some notion of what His powers may really be, but it affords no index to "the express image of His Person." There are a few general attributes to be assigned to His "image," as the term is used in Holy Scripture, which may be considered without offending against the ineffable majesty of His person. The "image of God" in which He made us, is an image that is—

I. *Rightful.*—It belongs to us as God's sons and daughters; it is our noblest heritage and birthright. Satan tried to take it away from man, and so to despoil and defile it, that its chief characters might be lost; but Jesus Christ came into the world to restore it to man again. It is, alas, easily defaced. A small fragment chipped out of the marble alters the entire contour of the features. One unrepented and habitual sin changes the features of this spiritual image in a complete and wonderful manner. We all dislike to be defrauded of our money, our fair fame, our position, our possessions, and our honours. Beyond all, let us dread the effects of sin, which defraud us of that likeness by which when we cry to God we can claim His parentage, saying, "Abba, Father."

II. *Glorious.*—How can it fail to be so, since it represents "the God of glory," Who is glorious in His holiness; in His works; in His power, wisdom, and knowledge; in His dealings with the children of men. God is glorious alike in His being and in His attributes; and therefore the image of Him must be, to some extent, representative of His glory. Look at this poor and lowly life; this frail, mortal body, subject to disease, decay, and death; filled with and tormented by many a sore ache and a dire pain, and then look within Thee. Consider, O man, thy soul; there lies a hidden glory; there is the image of God. Wretchedness and rags may greet the eye of man; within there is a sight which gladdens the eye of Angels. That poor despised one bears the glorious image of God within him.

III. *Perfect.*—There is no imperfection in God; nothing whatsoever wanting in Him; and there is nothing present with Him out of its due proportion. The finest work of art is more or less spoiled through some imperfection, either of form or of colour; the true image of God is absolutely perfect in its every detail. What fault can be found with the earthly life of Him in Whom God's image was so wonderfully and perfectly represented to man?

IV. *Enduring.*—" I am," " I change not ;" " from everlasting to everlasting Thou art God." All else may change but God and His image. Herein consists man's true immortality : he bears about with him the enduring image of God.

Epilogue.—Seek those divine graces by which this image of God can once more be restored to the soul.

Cultivate "industry" in holiness, faith, and prayer. Having gained that image, preserve it with all care. Let not sin defile it; protect it under every temptation of life; it will be its own passport to the spirit world after death, and adorn the glory of the resurrection.

SERMON V.
THE LAW OF SYMPATHY.

He did not many mighty works there because of their unbelief."
—*S. Matt.* xiii. 58.

Origen.—By these words we are taught that " mighty works " were wrought amongst the believing; since, ' Whosoever hath, to him shall be given, and he shall have more abundance ' (S. Matt. xiii. 12); but amongst the unbelieving He not only did no ' mighty works,' but as S. Mark writes, He could not do any: ' He could do there no mighty work ' (S. Mark vi. 6); for he does not say that He was unwilling, but ' He could ' not; as if in doing a ' mighty work,' help comes from the faith of him upon whom it was being wrought, and that it could be hindered by unbelief. Note, that He replied to those asking, ' Why could not we cast him out ?' ' Because of your unbelief.' (S. Matt. xvii. 19, 20.) To Peter beginning to sink He said, ' O thou of little faith, wherefore didst thou doubt ?' (S. Matt. xiv. 31.) (Also cases of S. Luke viii. 43; S. Matt. xvi. 20.) It seems to me that as in corporal things, agriculture is not sufficient for the formation of fruit unless the surrounding air works together to this end, or rather He ordaining the nature and quality of the air as He wills it; neither also does the air, without agriculture, or rather without Him Who foresees, cause the things which grow out of the earth to grow without agriculture. Once He caused this to happen by these words, "Let the earth bring forth grass, the herb yielding seed, etc." (Gen. i. 11.) Neither do the operations of 'mighty works,' without the faith of them who are healed, produce a perfect work of healing; nor can earth do this, let it be by what kind soever it may, without the Divine power."—*Comment. in Matt. Huet.* vol. i. pp. 226, C; 227, B.

Our Blessed Lord had all power to work miracles, and no human creature could stay or hold His Almighty hand; yet He willed to be so stayed from performing many a deed of love and mercy, unless there was some sympathy between the Worker and those on whose behalf He worked. Jesus Christ connected His miracles with the faith of man, to show the operation in its full force of the law of Sympathy. He taught the lesson that men must feel with Him, if they willed that He should work for them. Hence

His Gospel is one of love and sympathy, as contrasted with the old Law of reward and punishment. As in other particulars, so also in sympathy did the Lord become to us a "Pattern Man." This sympathy, fellow-suffering with another, or fellow affection for him, is in its nature—

I. *Subtle.*—It cannot be strictly defined; it comes to the soul as an instinct, rather than as a sense that can be corrected or developed. 1) It is felt even before the grounds for such feeling are realized, so sudden is it in its coming. Without preparation, without warning, it takes possession of the soul. 2) It penetrates at once to the secret chamber of the heart, awakening unto new life a faculty which may have long lain unknown or undiscovered there. 3) It selects its own point of contact, and holds fast by it, even when the sympathetic nature becomes as it were a circle to another nature, which can only touch it at one point of contact. 4) Against the will itself; against many a previous anticipation of antagonism it asserts its silent sway. It in a moment converted Saul the Persecutor into "Paul the Servant of Jesus Christ."

II. *Binding.*—Sympathy when once established can very rarely be broken off. It may be denied an active manifestation, but it lies no less securely at the root of the affections. It may receive many a rude shock, but only in the extremest cases is it severed. It binds soul with soul. 1) Unselfishly; it is a complete and entire going out of self, which is forgotten in the thought and care for another. Sympathy with the sufferings of Jesus makes the Christian unmindful of his own petty cares and sorrows; he rather goes out of himself to sympathize in spirit with his suffering and sorrowing Lord. 2) Closely; it is no mere liking for, or appreciation of, but the highest and most intense form of feeling with the one upon whom it is exercised. No true holiness can exist without sympathy, which makes "the mind of Jesus Christ" become another's mind, and the life of Jesus Christ another's life. 3) Lastingly; it is the product, sometimes of a moment, producing a lifelong effect; which survives in many cases the power to give it active expression. In old age even, keen and bright as when first appealing to the heart of youth; like love, sympathy is verily stronger than death.

III. *Influencing.*—Sympathy frequently asserts its superiority to the will, proving that the heart is stronger than the head, influencing the whole inner man. It influences—1) the judgment; hence it is so difficult to form any judgment upon another that is strictly just; that is not influenced by the opposing forces of either sympathy or antipathy. Sympathy, called into active exercise for or against a cause, doctrine, or person, seldom allows the reason to take its legitimate share in the formation of opinion. 2) The course of life. Sustained by sympathy, we can bear much, that without it would almost press down the soul to death. It may afford no material aid, yet in spite of this its help is often very real. Its entire solitariness must have formed no small item in the unspeakable Passion of our Lord. It is a stern fact of death, the having to die alone. 3) The perfection of truth. Sympathy is demanded for any writer or mind, before that writer or mind can be understood and appreciated. It is because men have so little sympathy with things divine that the mysteries of the faith are so little known, understood, and cared for. To awaken intellectual sympathy is the one great object of education ; to awaken spiritual sympathy is the one great object of faith.

IV. *Exciting.*—Sympathy awakens in the soul new desires, aspirations, emotions, hopes ; it stimulates the soul to new and increased exertions ; it draws out many a faculty, the existence of which was before unknown. 1) It kindles a new life in the heart, breeding a host of fresh feelings, and unlocking many an affection well nigh frozen. 2) It enlarges the sphere of both thought and action, making its horizon commensurate with its own growth. 3) It adapts to its own good uses and purposes many a means before unrecognized; many an opportunity before unheeded.

Epilogue.—There is a sympathy with evil as well as with good; with all that is basest and devilish in our lowly nature, as well as with all that is best and holiest. There is a sympathy to be shunned and stamped out of the soul, as well as one to be fostered and tended. It is a mighty power for weal or for woe. If the want of a righteous sympathy could hinder the work of Jesus Christ in the flesh, see that the want of such sympathy hinders not the work of His Spirit in the heart. In sympathy with all that is Christlike, good, and great, man regains his lost heritage on earth, and will inherit a new and better Paradise of God when called upon to sit in "heavenly places with Christ Jesus."

SERMON VI.
THE STRONG MAN OF DOUBT.

"How can one enter into a strong man's house, and spoil his goods, except he first bind the strong man? and then he will spoil his house."—*S. Matt.* xii. 29.

Origen.—"First, therefore, is the strong man bound and restrained by the bands of questions, and then the entering in, to the spoiling of his goods and the liberation of the souls which he had possessed by the fraud of deceit."—*In Ex. Hom.* iv. *Geneb.* vol. i. p. 43, E.

"The strong man" well represents those doubts which at times assail every earnest soul; and the "goods" which he retains in his possession, are the affections, with the graces of faith, love, fear, and hope. "The souls which he had possessed," well represent the several powers and faculties of the mind. To some, doubt is indeed a "strong man," who has taken possession of all that is best and holiest in them; who has eaten out all the noblest elements of their life and character; has paralyzed every earnest endeavour; has destroyed every ardent aspiration and

The Strong Man of Doubt. 27

hope. How then can this strong man be overcome? This is a matter of the gravest moment, and a great master of the spiritual life answers that he is to be "bound and restrained by questions;" that is, by a rigorous examination of the ground upon which he bases his claims, so that when they are thoroughly sifted and examined his falsely-gained possessions may be wrested from him again. These "questions" by which the strong man of doubt is bound and restrained must be—

I. *Searching.*—A cursory or half-inspection of a complex title-deed would lead to no results. A casual glance of doubt would not solve any of its difficulties; it must be "bound and restrained" by questions which reach to the depths of—1) Faith. Upon what is faith grounded? Exists there a revelation from God to man? Is there a Mediator and Redeemer Who must stand between the soul and God? Are there supernatural channels of grace conveyed from heaven to earth in the Sacraments of the Church? If the Christian faith be rejected, can it be replaced by another equally credible, equally suited to man's needs, equally appealing to that which is best and highest in his nature? 2) Life. What is the mystery of man's being? By whom and for whom was man created? What is the final cause and purpose in man's existence? Has not every creature a determined and pre-ordained mission to sustain and course to run? What is my course and mission? 3) Experience. What are the lessons which I learn from the past days of my life? Have they taught me that there are such things as providence, conscience, rewards, and punishments; certain moral and spiritual laws which have been implanted in the soul by a most wise and most just Great First Cause of all things? The past is full of lessons, and it testifies most abundantly to the ordering of all things by One Who is alike the God of nature and of grace.

II. *Solemn.* —Not to be asked in a careless way, as if their answer one way or the other was as a matter of no moment. An eternity hangs upon their answer; an everlasting existence of either happiness or misery; heaven or hell; as well as our present peace. They must be asked in a spirit which is not—1) frivolous; inclined to jest at or to lightly treat holy things. 2) Supercilious; as being above and beyond all law and conditions of life, and therefore impressed with a lofty contempt for all who trouble themselves about their final and lasting estate. 3) Indifferent; as if it mattered nothing whether the answer was for or against; involving no issues about which the soul need seriously concern itself.

III. *Thoughtful.*—An expression of every lurking difficulty and doubt which may be in the obscurest recesses of the soul; framed to meet the particular bent or habit of mind of the propounder. They must represent a mind taking counsel with itself, and disputing with itself concerning the faith. These questions should bring into action the whole power of the—1) Understanding; in order that the question may be fairly, and in all particulars, placed before the mind. 2) Reason ; that the consequences and deductions from each argument may be rightly estimated. 3) Memory; that no part of the argument may be lost sight of during the flow of thought. 4) Will; that all the powers of the mind may be concentrated upon and directed to the one single topic under review.

IV. *Plain.*—The " strong man " of doubt is surely to be bound by questions which are plain in their— 1) askings. No uncertain sound or meaning must be left to lurk in the impression which they convey to the mind. They must be brought out in the simplest and clearest manner possible. 2) Answers. A clear question can hardly fail to beget a clear response ; short, often nothing more than a yes or no ; and yet all the more direct from this very brevity. 3) Consequences or deductions. Upon such deductions the solution of the larger number of the problems of life depend. More than half the error and misunderstanding in the world arises from a certain want of clearness of expression, which both engenders and fosters doubt.

Epilogue.—May we, by earnest, prayerful examination of soul first, be so enabled to bind "the strong man of doubt," that we may recover those goods of which, from time to time, he has so basely robbed us, and so rejoice in the liberty wherewith Jesus has made us free.

SERMON VII.

IMPRESSIONS.

" A good man out of the good treasure of the heart bringeth forth good things ; and an evil man out of the evil treasure bringeth forth evil things."—*S. Matt.* xii. 35.

Origen.—" Every man has some food within himself which he can yield to his neighbour coming to him. For it is not possible when we men have approached each other and joined in discourse, that we have not given or received some taste either from an answer or a question or from some other sign. And if he, indeed, is a pure man and of a good mind from whom we take the taste, we take good food; but if he is impure whom we lay hold of, the food is impure."—*Geneb.* vol. i. p. 87, D. E. *In Levit. Hom.* vii.

We are ever receiving " tastes " or impressions from those by whom we are surrounded. The stronger mind acts unconsciously upon the weaker; and a word uttered in jest, an opinion often expressed at random, a statement which is bold, but unfounded, sinks into the mind and colours the whole tenor of the life. In our common intercourse, in our daily conversation, we are feeding perpetually, either for good or for ill, the minds of others. Never does a conversation pass in which we do not receive " some taste " or impression which abides in the memory long after the subject of the conversation itself is lost sight of and forgotten. The earthly recorded life of the Lord is full of " tastes " or impressions which are the result of His particular action, word, and dealing all combined. His blessed life as a whole, as well as every special portion of it conveys an impression or "taste" which brings a holy and soothing remembrance with it. We note that these impressions are often—

I. *Sudden.*—They are conveyed to the mind in a moment of time. Quicker than the course of lightning does the soul seize upon them; so quickly that their leaven is already at work ere the mind is conscious of their reception. The understanding does not stay to analyse, it accepts the impression at once; it imbibes the taste without effort, without consideration. The mind resembles the prepared plate upon which the image mirrored by the camera is impressed almost instantaneously. This sudden impressiveness should make us—1) Watchful; guarding the soul with all diligence. 2) Well-grounded in our faith and principles, so as not easily to be led away. 3) Candid and open, that no occasion from which we may derive profit, spiritual, moral, or intellectual, may escape us. Spiritual discernment will enable the mind to sift the bad from the good, without any effort of thought.

II. *Delicate.*—" Tastes " or impressions are frequently the result of a combination of causes, of some indirect action upon the soul. They are formed upon one deed or word, but are the product of a thousand reflections, associations, and memories, all combined. Our impression of character is usually a summary of all the qualities which we have noted in the person subject to thought. Hence we should be—1) Cautious in allowing too strong a place to our own likes and dislikes, since another's mind is as the moon when seen by us at its fulness; there is still a half of it in darkness on the other side beyond our range of vision. 2) Cautious in tampering for interested motives with an impression which our spiritual or moral sense knows and feels to be a true one. Such an impression is a case of conscience. 3) Cautious in trying to reduce to hard rule and rigid outline the somewhat misty though true and delicate impression which the mind may have justly received.

III. *Powerful.*— Our whole life is under the dominion of one or other sets of impressions, since it is these which give us our likes and dislikes; which determine our line of life and action; our hope, faith, love, desire, aim, and final cause in all that we are, or in all that we are seeking to become. Very powerful are they, and they rule us—1) Unconsciously: we know not the motive power by which we are guided, yet none the less surely are we walking under its guidance. 2) Irresistibly: they are no tangible enemies with which we can fight, against which we can struggle; they form a part of our very selves and of our lives. 3) Universally: there is no portion of our mind or conduct which is left untouched or uninfluenced by them.

IV. *Lastingly.*—The " taste " or impression which is so sudden that it is formed in a moment, may last throughout life, and perhaps abide with the soul in eternity for ever. In this, as in other respects, the action of an instant carries with it an eternal consequence. Through all the changes, joys, sorrows, temptations, victories, and defeats of life, the one impression remains, unbroken, unsubdued. This consideration makes our impressions to be solemn in their—1) Continuance; abiding ever, still the same. 2) Consequence; knowing no determinate period of effacement. 3) Connection with all that is real and vital as concerning this world and the next.

Epilogue.—As givers, of "tastes" or impressions, the Lord's words in the text have a grand force;

warning me, lest by my action, word, or deed, a false impression may lead my brother's soul astray. As receivers, to take this saying of Jesus as a touchstone and a warning by which every spirit may be tried, to see whether or not it be of God.

SERMON VIII.
THE ETERNAL RECORD.

"My wound is grievous."—*Jer.* x. 19.

Origen.—"In the wounds of the body, after they have been cured, there sometimes remains the mark of the wound itself, which is called a scar. It is hardly ever so cured that no trace of the received wound is seen to remain. Pass now from this shadow of the law to its truth, and mark how the soul which has received the wound of sin, even if it be cured, has the scar of sin remaining in the place of the wound, which, although cured, bears still the indication of the old wound in the traces itself of the scar."—*In Levit. Hom.* viii. *Geneb.* vol. i. p. 90, M; p. 91, A.

It has been established by philosophers that motion is imperishable, and that the vibrations of every spoken word last for ever. An infinite intelligence can read aright all the aerial undulations that have been formed by man from Adam's day to our own. Hence the act of speech, to the Divine Mind, carries with itself its own eternal record. Again, light, rapid as it is, still takes time to travel. As God removes His source of vision further from this earth, so does He see that which has been done upon it in time past. If the inhabitant of a star of remote magnitude could behold this world he would see it as it was before man appeared on the scene at all; or coming nearer, he could see Adam walking with Eve in Paradise. Thus the omniscience of God can be explained by His omnipresence. Thus the very light itself, rapid as is its course, carries an eternal record of our acts from the cradle to the grave. Lastly. The heart is allowed by many to be its own witness, as bearing its own eternal record of every thought, whether for good or for evil, which has ever passed over its surface. It was the greatest uninspired mind which the world had ever known who insisted most strongly upon the fact, that the mind or soul was its own eternal witness to all the thoughts which it had ever conceived—it being a book in which it chronicles its own thoughts. (Plato. Phil. 58, E.) In the case of pardoned sin, the scar or mark of former wounds and suffering remains. The Lord is still pleading by his five most sacred wounds, living streams of grace and mercy for us men who are encompassed with so many infirmities of sin and sorrow. The scars of conquered sin are more noble than even the medals which the brave soldier wears. Scars may be also the last remains of a past dishonour, and may serve to keep their possessor humble even in the midst of glory. Standing around the throne of the great King we shall still feel some sense of shame at bearing so many traces of our former sin. Each scar becomes a living monument of God's great grace and mercy towards us. Of these scars of sin we note that they are—

I. *Memorial.*—They bring our past state and the former events of life before the memory. The scars of the sacred hands and feet and side of Jesus recall to Him throughout eternity the life of suffering which He led here on earth ; they never allow Him to forget for one single instant that which for our sake He once endured. The scars or marks which the soul will bear in Heaven will remind us—1) Of a former condition, when we were under the powerful influences of temptation and sin. They will for ever mark the epoch of our lowly walking in this present imperfect state and life. 2) Of our healing and deliverance through the infinite love and mercy of our dear Lord. 3) Of the mighty contrast between this glorious present and the saddened past which went before it.

II. *True.*—Not a trace of any false witness will be found in the evidence which they give. They were graven on the heart by our own thoughts; they are the evidences of that which once found a place there. In number also they will be not one scar too many, not one too few. They are wholly and absolutely true in their—1) Number. Like the register of a turnstile they record a just number of falls, repentances, seasons of doubt and of faith, of hate and love. 2) Character. Some scars are larger, deeper, uglier than others, according as the sins and conflicts have been more less mortal and severe. 3) In order and succession. Some scars will be found to overlap others, as the successive growth of an exogenous tree is recorded by rings of an increasing diameter. No ground of complaint against them on the score of their want of fidelity can stand.

III. *Voluntary.*—Not in their presence and inscription, but in the causes whence they sprang. A large portion of our sinful thoughts it is in our power, by the prayerful use of Divine grace, to hinder. The more we give way to evil thoughts, desires, and inclinations, the larger will be the number of those scars which will bear their eternal record against us. We all could have saved many a scar by resisting—1) the temptations and insinuations of sin in thought; 2) the occasions of sin in act; 3) the agony and struggle which must ever follow true repentance after a fall. It will be through carelessness and effeminacy, through obstinacy and hardness of heart, that many a soul is now, during this present life, being scarred and marked.

IV. *Indelible.*—They can never be blotted out. No after tears, no final glory, will either wash them entirely away or gild them over. They will remain, and form for ever an eternal chronicle of time. They will be indelible in—1) Their presence; never to be got rid of. 2) Their witness; silent, yet patent to God and ourselves. 3) Their effects upon those who know of no escape from their mark.

Epilogue.—These thoughts suggest—1) an increased holiness and prayerfulness of life ; 2) the near relations which exist between time and eternity; 3) the use of sacramental grace to purify the soul.

SERMON IX.
THE GARDENER.

"She, supposing Him to be the gardener."*—*S. John* xx. 15.

Origen.—" Oh ! Mary ! if you seek Jesus, why do you not know Him ? And if you know Jesus, why do you seek Him ? Behold ! Jesus comes to thee, and He Whom you seek asks of thee, ' Woman, why weepest thou ?' and you, not knowing Him, suppose ' Him to be the gardener.' For He is Jesus, and a Gardener, since He Himself sows every good seed in the garden of thy soul, and in the hearts of His faithful ones. He plants and waters all the good herbs in the souls of the holy, and it is Jesus Himself Who speaks with thee."—*Hom.* x. *De Diver. Geneb.* vol. ii. p. 293, E.

In explaining the Parable of the Tares the Lord Himself said, " He that soweth the good seed is the

---

* " The Gardener and His Garden." Reading XVIII. in Dr. Neale's " Sermons for Children," is a beautiful exposition of this same thought. Fourth Edition (Hayes), pp. 127-133.

Son of Man." (S. Matt. xiii. 37.) Since whatsoever good things are produced in the soul of man are from the Word which was "in the beginning with God." (S. John i. 2.) (*Origen in loco.*) The human application of a garden or vineyard is beautifully made by the Prophets of old. (Isa. v. 1-7 ; Jer. xii. 10 : Micah i. 6.) In fact a garden is no inapt similitude of the soul of which Jesus Christ, as the Lord of souls, is the Gardener. The consideration of this similitude involves a reflection upon—

I. *The Gardener.*—Jesus Christ may well be called the Gardener of the garden of the human soul, since this garden—1) He owns. It is His own garden. He does not tend it for hire, for the good of others, but for Himself. Jesus bought this garden at the price of His most precious blood. It was in the possession of God at first ; then Satan obtained it by craft ; lastly Jesus Christ became Incarnate, lived and died that He might redeem this garden, and obtain it for Himself for ever. 2) He loves. Jesus may have richer and fairer domains, more costly and magnificent possessions, but He loves this poor garden of the soul with the deepest, tenderest, fondest love. It was the one object of His thoughts when He dwelt in heaven at the right hand of God ; during the time of His earthly sojourn ; now and for ever whilst He is seated at the "right hand of the Majesty on high." Love is careful, watchful, and jealous; so—3) He tends this garden with an anxious solicitude, lest harm should happen to it; rank weeds grown up in it—deadly weeds of sin; lest the walls of it should be broken down; the barriers of belief give way, and so the garden become a wilderness of confusion and of doubt. May we be led to value this garden of the soul at the same high price at which the Saviour Himself valued it!

II. *The Garden.*—This garden of the soul is—1) fruitful. The soil of the soul is most productive; it is ever bringing forth. The harvest and fruit-gathering season will determine both the nature and the value of its produce. The soul is no wilderness; it never can be wholly barren; if not productive of good it must be productive of evil. It is a fruitful garden, whether for heaven or for hell. 2) Pleasing. A garden in good order and cultivation is always a pleasing object. Nature and art are working together towards the same end, and the combination suggests a sense of prosperity, progress, and peace. The garden of the soul, tended by the love and care of Jesus Christ, and watered by the Holy Ghost, affords a fair scene upon which the eye may well rest content. Sad when this fruitful place becomes a desolation; covered with a rank overgrowth of evil habits and desires. 3) Profitable. It bears fruit not for time only but also for eternity ; fruit, the use and value of which we are unable to gauge and measure here. May the gardens of our souls be productive in heavenly, pleasing, and eternally profitable fruit; bearing much fruit, and so being worthy of all the loving care and attention of the Gardener.

III. *The flowers of the garden.*—With such a Gardener and so rich a soil, a like richness and diversity ought to be found in the flowers which grow therein. Amongst the flowers which must flourish there, if the garden would please the Heavenly Gardener, we note the—1) white lily of purity, with graceful stem and large creamy petals ; stately yet modest ; beautiful yet unobtrusive. This is a flower which both adorns the garden and consecrates all the other flowers there. Without the Christian grace of purity no other graces can avail, or glorify by their proper colours the beauty of the garden. 2) Snowdrop, of hope and consolation ; delicate, tender head of bell-shaped petals, peeping trustingly out of the snow-covered ground. Many a season of winter or sorrow in every life when the emblem of the time of a future summer of joy is grateful indeed. 3) Ivy of fidelity ; which clings for support to the old faith of the ages, inserting its roots into the very structure of the Church, and gaining a new life and vigour from its association with the old. 4) Syringa of memory, with its lovely scent, strongest at eventide; ministering to the close of the day, as memory does to the close of life. 5) Canary-grass of perseverance; often uprooted, with small hold upon the soil, yet still existing, and not to be destroyed and eradicated. The soul is often sorely tried; and weak, bending down to the storm with, it may be, a small hold upon the mysteries of the faith, yet never wholly giving way; maintaining against fearful odds its own hold upon things divine. 6) Ox-eye of penitence, which flows from that plain, stern examination of self, which reveals imperfection, and casts the soul upon God's mercy for pardon and for peace. 7) Moss-rose of love, with its red opening and scented petals; fit emblem of that refreshing fire of love which warms up all the inner man; which consumes indwelling sin, and unites man's spirit with the cherubim. Such are a few of the flowers which, growing in the garden of the soul, are cherished and tended by the heavenly Gardener.

Epilogue.—What are the plants which are growing in the garden of your soul? There are plants of evil as well as of good. May—1) the evil plants be rooted up (S. Matt. xv. 13); 2) the good plants multiply; 3) the heavenly Gardener rejoice in His garden of your heart.

SERMON X.

THE MIDDLE WAY.

"I am the way."—*S. John* xiv. 6.

Origen.—"Let us therefore, declining neither to the right hand nor to the left, walk in the middle way, which is the Lord Christ, since the Lord directeth the steps of those who walk in Him."—*Hom.* iii. *in Psal.* xxxvi., *Geneb.* vol. i. p. 285, F.

Besides being "the way" to heaven, our Blessed Lord came down to earth to be "the way" to man during his present life on earth. The teaching and the life of Jesus Christ alike point Him out to us as giving us a "middle way" in which we should strive to walk in this our middle state between the past and the future; between non-existence and final glory. The earthly life of Jesus Christ, which is our pattern life, was truly a "middle way" between—

I. *Humiliation and glory.*—A lowly birth of lowly parents; a poor, hard life; homeless and houseless; an ignominious death; these stood between the choirs of Angels who chanted out His Christmas hymn; His

Divine power; the glory of His Transfiguration; His Resurrection and Ascension. The outward life of the Lord was one of sore humiliation; the inner life, one of perpetual and sustained glory, which was but rarely manifested. So also is the Christian life one of humiliation flowing from—1) A sense of sin and of weakness; 2) want of sympathy with the world and the world's ways; 3) the daily sacrifice of the present to the future. The Christian walks humbly as in the presence of a higher Power; as ever surrounded by a spirit world which encloses him on all sides; as having the end and just reward of life constantly before his eyes. Yet is this humiliation, tempered with some few faint rays of that glory which shall be revealed in him hereafter, since he carries about with him the means of—1) Spiritual conquest. He is ever striving and often overcoming. Each victory over sin adds new lustre to his future crown. 2) Divine grace; which helps his infirmities, endows him with new and peculiar powers, adorning his soul with many a heavenly attribute. 3) Future perfection. This the Christian feels most strongly; although now I am greatly unworthy, I shall be most worthy by-and-by. When all false appearances shall have for ever passed away, then shall I shine as the sun in the firmament of my Heavenly Father's Kingdom. Thus the holy life, humble as it really is, contains the seeds of all exaltation within it. It is a "middle way" between humiliation and final glory.

II. *Joy and Sorrow.*—The life or "middle way" of Jesus Christ was one of sorrow. He was emphatically the "man of sorrows" (Isa. liii. 3); sorrowing over all that He gave up for the sake of man; over the seeming failure of His earthly mission (S. John i. 11) ; over the ingratitude, distrust, and coldness which was so often His sad portion whilst ministering to men ; over the bitter death which He knew was before Him. (S. Luke xii. 50 ; S. Matt. xxvi. 38.) Behind this outward garb of sorrow there must have been a deep, inextinguishable joy in His heart. The Saviour could look beyond Calvary to Bethany; beyond Bethany to "the throne of His glory;" beyond the contradictions and narrow-mindedness of the Scribes and Pharisees of to-day, to the "regeneration" when in the midst of His redeemed the triumph of His saving love would assuredly be glorious and complete. So the Christian life is one of sorrow, for it is one of earnestness, and all earnest emotion in this present life is sad. He treads the sorrowful "Highway of the Holy Cross" in his—1) Self-discipline ; 2) Repentance; 3) Condemnation of an un-Christlike world. Yet he sorrows not without hope : it is a godly sorrow which he now bears; a sowing in tears, one day to reap in joy. Looking onwards and upwards,

The Middle Way. 49

he hears the whisper of his Lord saying, "Your joy," etc., (S. John xvi. 22.) The future consecrates the present, and he therefore rejoices—1) In the common blessings of daily life as being the gifts of his Heavenly Father. 2) In the beauties of creation; of moral goodness and of intellectual achievement. 3) In a calm sense of pardoned sin. 4) In the firm hope of future glory. His joy is deep, firm, and lasting; the world gave it not and therefore cannot take it away. The faithful soul treads the "middle way" between perfect joy and a sorrow without hope.

III. *Fear and Love.*—As Son of Man the Lord walked partly in fear of man (S. John vi. 15) and of God (S. Matt. xxvii. 46); yet love to both man and God was the one passion of His holy soul. During His earthly ministration His love was pent up and restrained. It showed more brightly after His resurrection; it will show in all its brightness when the Great Shepherd will be one day with His sheep; when there shall be no let or hindrance to the full exposition and outpouring of His love. Now, too, does the faithful soul walk along a "middle path" between a fear which leads to—1) Hopelessness and despair; 2) which paralyzes all effort; 3) which degrades man and dishonours God; and a love which is perfect—1) As casting out all fear; 2) as giving repose to the soul and so weakening the desire for further perfection; 3) as fulfilling the heavenly life whilst being still subject to the conditions of sin and death.

Epilogue.—The faithful soul, humbly walking along the "middle way" which the Lord trod before it, gains a threefold spirit of—1) Thankfulness. There has been a deliverance from the lowest estate of humiliation, sorrow, and fear. 2) Contentment. The present, not itself perfect, contains the germs of future perfection; it is a worthy walk, with high opportunities, promising great rewards. 3) Hope. The "middle way" will resolve itself into a way of perfect and eternal glory, joy, and love. Oh follow Jesus, along that "middle way." He beckons you to follow Him; He says, "I am the way."

SERMON XI.
THE RIGHT HEART.

"Thy heart is not right in the sight of God."—*Acts* viii. 21.

Origen.—"We know Simon Magus, proclaiming himself to be the 'Power of God,' that is, called great, fell away together with his silver to destruction and perdition."—*Comm. in Joan, Huet.*, vol. ii. p. 36, D.

"Simon Magus, the Samaritan, endeavoured to deceive certain persons by magic."—*Cont. Cel. lib.* i. sec. 57.

It is said that if the physician of the body had the power of observing every internal organism, he would discover something not "right" even in the healthiest subject; some small function of the human mechanism to be out of order, even in the strongest and most robust frame. If this be true of the body, how much more true must it be of the soul. The great Physician of souls, knowing "what is in man," must discern, not merely a trace of disease here and there, but souls innumerable full of spiritual "wounds bruises, and putrifying sores." A ghastly sight must the inspection of the souls of men present to Him, before Whom " all hearts are open." In the case of Simon Magus it was neither the head nor the body which was diseased, it was his heart which was " not right in the sight of God." There must have been much good in Simon; his character as represented in the inspired chronicle was not wholly bad. True, that he practised magic and sorcery; " that of a long time he had bewitched " the people of Samaria " with sorceries;" but his calling was a recognized one among the superstitious people with whom he lived, and at the particular age of the world in which he flourished. He was distinguished from a vast number of other sorcerers, chiefly by the extraordinary note and success that he gained in his profession. When, however, Simon Magus heard of the better life through the preaching of Philip, we find that—Firstly: He renounced his old calling, profitable and influential as it was; which renunciation must have cut him off from further increase of means; from many of his old associates, and given the lie to his former life. How many Christians would be willing to give up a means of livelihood in which they had been successful, for the sake of the honour and fealty which is due to Jesus Christ? Secondly: " He believed;" his mind was open to receive the impression and conviction of truth when it was brought before him. Such belief implied a candid and impressible mind. Thirdly: "He was baptized." Simon was neither ashamed to confess nor to profess his new faith. This act implied a certain amount of moral courage rarely to be met with, and worthy of all praise. Fourthly: "He continued with Philip" to learn the way of God more perfectly; to be more fully instructed in the mysteries of the faith. This fact implies a humble and docile disposition. Fifthly: After his unholy proposition had been denounced by S. Peter in language both strong and severe, Simon took the correction in a becoming spirit, still asserted his belief in the efficacy of prayer to S. Peter's God, and begged of the Apostle "to pray to the Lord" for him. From a sense of personal disappointment, mortification, or pique, he did not throw over his newly-embraced faith, and betake himself to his old trade of sorcery again. Simon Magus committed a grievous sin, and fell, as many a better man than he had fallen before him; but not on that account is he worthy of unmitigated reprobation. The fall of Simon shows but too plainly that there was something radically wrong about him; and what that something is, S. Peter revealed in the solemn words: "Thy heart is not right in the sight of God." Simon was in the main "right in the head," he was, alas! wholly wrong in the heart, being "still in the gall of bitterness and the bond of iniquity." Even his very desire to buy "the gift of God, with money," was an evidence of true faith living within the man. It showed that he was willing to part with his material substance, if by such loss he could receive some spiritual gain. The power of conferring the Holy Ghost was more to him than the possession of so much silver. Herein it must be acknowledged that a sixth trait of goodness appears in his disposition; one in addition to those which have been already enumerated. Like the young man in the Gospel, Simon Magus was "not far from the Kingdom of God;" whilst his request most clearly revealed the fact, that despite his self-sacrifice, his baptism, his sojourn with holy Philip, he had not actually entered into that mysterious, invisible, and spiritual world which is designated by the title of the "Kingdom of God."

As far then as his head was concerned, Simon Magus was not so very far wrong. The failure and the cause of ill was certainly to be traced to his heart, which "was not right in the sight of God." This want of rectitude in the heart arose doubtless from its not being—

I. *Sanctified by God's Grace.*—As the soul grows in holiness, so does it grow in a keen sense of its own sin and unworthiness in particular, and in a special and acute sense of sin in general. Had Simon Magus been sanctified by the grace of God, he would have been so humbled under a sense of his own unworthiness, that he would have refused this Divine gift had it been freely offered to him; he would have felt himself unfit for its possession. The working of holiness would have deepened to an almost infinite degree the contrast between his own heart and the Spirit of Truth. Reverence for the mysteries of the Kingdom of God increases in proportion to that holiness which—1) brings them nigh to the heart; 2) conforms the heart to them; 3) gives the heart possession of them.

II. *Enlightened by God's Spirit.*—The eye o' faith, when enlightened by God's grace, far outstrips the mental or intellectual vision; faith being above reason. Simon had an intellectual conception of the teaching of Philip, but he lacked spiritual enlightenment. Of this need (1 Cor. ii. 11) his case was not that of (Eph. i. 18); hence he was not fully alive in respect of this spiritual gift which he desired, to its—1) Sacredness; embodying the very Person of God the Holy Ghost. 2) Power; influencing for eternity souls made after God's own image and likeness. 3) Glory; bringing God down to man; heaven to earth; light to darkness; purity to sin; life to death. The sacredness, power, and glory of the Sacraments of the Church can only be fully realized by those eyes God hath opened.

III. *Touched by God's Love.*—Had (Rom. v. 5) this very shedding abroad been present, it would have filled Simon with holy fear. That perfect love of God which casteth out all fear, belongs more properly to the future state of glory than to the present state of imperfection; belongs to the very few, alas, who have made their calling and election sure. True love renders the heart—1) Sensitive; fearful in all things of offence. 2) Diffident of its own power of winning and receiving. 3) Jealous of the honour of the loved one. True love must have stayed Simon Magus from his unholy request.

Epilogue.—God says, " Give Me," not thy mind, but " thy heart." (Prov. xxiii. 26.) Give God thy heart then, if that be " right," accepted by Him; all else will be " right " for time and for eternity, every thought, word, and deed.

SERMON XII.

HEAVEN OUR PERFECTION.

"Zion, the perfection of beauty."—*Ps.* l. 2.

Origen.—"For neither is this world able to apprehend that which is perfect wherein the necessity of the body suggests, now food, now drink, now sleep; all of which things, without doubt, interrupt the continuity of the festival of God."—*In Numb. Hom.* xxiii. *Geneb.* vol. i. p. 165, B.

Graver imperfections are attached to the soul and the state of life; but Zion is the perfection not of beauty alone, but of every form of it which stands in contrast with this imperfect and changing world.

In contrast then with earth and this present life we note in Heaven a state of perfect and absolute—

I. *Justice.*—In this world it often seems that God's providence is apparently eminently unjust. Some have such an easy path in life before them: being born to honours, riches, luxuries, and refinements of all kinds; whilst the lot of others is hard, very hard.

Some are blessed with health, beauty, and strength; others are subject to perpetual weakness, deformity, disease. Some are very highly gifted; others are destitute of all gifts and graces. The whole history of man is a repetition of that of Dives and Lazarus on its every page. A place of reparation and restitution must remain for man beyond the grave. For the worn and weary, the miserable and the depressed, the feeble and the outcasts of this lowly existence, there remains a "bosom of Abraham" in which God's providence will be fully seen and His justice entirely vindicated. Heaven is the abode of righteousness or justice.

II. *Freshness.*—In this world man is ordained to labour either in mind or in body; this labour is absolutely needed to develope man's power; it is as essential to his development as the constant movements and restlessness of very little children is an important factor in their growth; but here all labour is attended with weariness, sometimes with infirmity and pain. In heaven there will be ceaseless energy and operation combined with the feeling of perfect rest. Freshness and activity go hand in hand. Glorious state to be for ever doing and yet to be able ever to do.

III. *Joy.*—It is one great mark of imperfection, that there is no such thing as pure, unmixed joy in this world; an element of sadness tinges our brightest moments, and dims the lustre of earth's greatest glories. All earthly joy is stained with some—1) actual pain, as painful remembrances; 2) want, which renders it incomplete; 3) saddening thought, such as that so very soon it will pass away.

IV. *Immortality.*—Earth is but a temporary resting-place; an inn, not a home. Hence earth is imperfect in—1) Its ties, so soon to be snapped asunder. The nearest and dearest ties of earth last but for the shortest time. The ties in heaven are as immortal as is our own nature. 2) Its works. Man often does much in the thirty or forty years of his life, during which he has had very many hindrances. What work can be carried on throughout the immortality of heaven? 3) It is ever tending to a future; imperfect in its present. In heaven time is not—past, present, future are blended into one perfect whole.

Epilogue.—Strive, by the help of Divine grace, so to combat with the imperfection of sin here as to rejoice to enter upon a state of heavenly perfection hereafter.

SERMON XIII.
PERFECT FAITH.

"Many believed in His Name when they saw the miracles which He did. But Jesus did not commit Himself unto them."—*S. John* ii. 23, 24.

Origen.—" Some one may ask why ' Jesus did not commit Himself unto them,' of whom it had been witnessed that they believed. Because it is said not to those who believe ' in Him ' Jesus did not commit Himself, but to those who believed ' in His Name.' It is one thing to believe ' in Him,' another thing to believe ' in His Name.' Therefore, he who through faith is not condemned, is not condemned because he believes ' in Him,' not because he believes ' in His Name.' For the Lord says, ' He that believeth in Me is not condemned,' but not he that believeth ' in My Name' is not condemned. Many are said to believe not ' in Him,' but ' in His Name.' They only who believe ' in Him ' are they who walk along the narrow and straight way leading to life, which is therefore found by few."—*In Evang. Joan. tom.* xi.; *Geneb.* vol. ii. p. 211, C. D.

At His last as well as at His first Passover many believed "in His Name;" they shouted out, "Hosanna to the Son of David" (S. Matt. xxi. 9) in one breath, and in another, "Crucify Him." The belief "in the Name" soon vanished: it had no real hold upon either life or heart; it expressed little, it led to no result. It is possible to believe "in the names" of many who are to us nothing more than names; who are associated with us by no ties; who are incapable of exercising any action upon us. It is a barren, dead faith which finds expression in the belief in a mere name. Something more than this is required. It was because Jesus Christ "knew what was in man" (S. John ii. 25), that He would not "commit Himself" to those merely who "believed in His Name." Perfect faith believes "in Him;" and such faith is—

I. *Personal*—To meet the needs of our own personality we require a personal Saviour, and our Lord fulfils this requisition, being a "High Priest Who is touched with the feeling of our infirmities" (Heb. iv. 14); hence He can have "compassion upon the ignorant and upon those who are out of the way" (Heb. v. 2) of hope, help, life, and joy. As a profession we may believe in a name; as a support and direction for life we must believe in a person. Our Blessed Lord therefore comes to us as a Friend, and more than a Friend; as the Elder Brother of our race; as bone of our bone and flesh of our flesh. This belief in the Person of Jesus Christ makes Him—1) Near. Although He is God, yet is He through participation of our common nature very nigh unto us. 2) Visible. We can see Jesus, and follow Him throughout every detail of His earthly life. 3) Familiar. There can be no familiarity, but fear and dread, in the contemplation of a spirit. (Job iv. 16.) Such a personal faith in Jesus appeals to all the higher and better faculties of our nature. He is a Person holy and divine; and as such He exercises a holy and divine influence upon the soul and life.

II. *Loving.*—It is next to impossible to love a mere name; to feel affection for an abstraction. There was much that was good, true, and beautiful in the religions of the world before the Gospel came into it; but they all failed in their mission, because they appealed to the intellect and the understanding rather than to the affections; they influenced the head rather than the heart. Jesus Christ drew men to Himself by "the cords of a man and by the bands of love." (Hos. xi. 4.) Hence, the more He is loved the more is He believed in; and the more He is believed in the more He is loved. Faith and love are united in the Loving Person of Jesus Christ. This loving faith becomes the true source of—1) Obedience. In all things the will of the loved one passes into law. It goes hard with the heart to disappoint or to displease one who is tenderly and truly loved. 2) Imitation. "Be ye followers of Christ as dear children." (Eph. v. 1.) Imitation begets likeness; likeness begets union; and union is perfected in final glory. 3) Joy. The command, "Rejoice in the Lord" (Phil. iv. 4), can only be fulfilled in those who believe in that Lord with a faith which worketh by love. (Gal. v. 6.)

III. *Experimental.*—The multitudes at both the first and last Passovers who believed "in the Name" of Jesus Christ had made no trial of their faith. It had stood them in no stead in their seasons of sin, sorrow, and weakness. Such had never tasted how gracious the Lord is. Experimental faith in a name must needs be small indeed; it wants a person either by himself or by his influence to comfort the sorrowful, strengthen the weak, awaken the sinner, and heal the soul-sick. Experimental faith in Jesus Christ finds Him—1) Willing to help man. The promise, "I will, be thou clean," applies to every circumstance of life. 2) Able, as being stronger than sin, death, and hell. 3) Actually exerting this willing power on behalf of all who humbly seek the blessed help. Hence His invitation. (S. Matt. xi. 28.) Make trial then of Him, and you cannot fail to believe in Him.

IV. *Living.*—The multitudes that "believed in His Name" had given no evidence of their faith. It had produced no fruits meet for repentance. (S. Matt. iii. 8.) The true disciple of the Lord says with the Apostle, "I will show thee my faith by my works." (S. James ii. 18.) Faith should so operate in the heart that all men may take knowledge of the faithful that they have been with Jesus. A living faith produces Christlike—1) Thoughts; 2) words: 3) deeds.

Epilogue.— So believe in the Person of Jesus Christ, that He may commit Himself to you wholly, continually, and eternally. (Rev. iii. 20.)

SERMON XIV.

THE SWORD OF TEACHING.

"I came not to send peace, but a sword."—*S. Matt.* x. 34.

Origen.—" For truly before He had descended, there was not a sword upon the earth, neither was the flesh lusting against the spirit, nor the spirit against the flesh. But when He came, and we had been taught the things which were of the flesh and of the spirit, THE TEACHING became as a sword in the earth, dividing the flesh and the earth from the spirit. And the earth indeed was exterminated, because we bear about in the body 'the dying of the Lord Jesus' (2 Cor. iv. 10); and we live no longer 'after the flesh' (Rom. viii. 1) but wholly to the spirit, lest of the flesh we should 'reap corruption.' (Gal. vi. 8.)—*Hom. in Jerem.* xi. *Huet.* vol. i. 113, B. C.

Man on earth is placed between two powers and kingdoms ; that of light and that of darkness : midway between heaven and hell ; between God and Satan : between absolute holiness and confirmed unpardonable sin. To neither state nor power was man as a race wholly allied; he was separate from God, yet he was not delivered up unconditionally to Satan. The Lord came to bring "peace on earth, to men of good will" (S. Luke ii. 14), by reconciling them to God; and "glory to God in the highest," in the salvation of man. Peace with God implies war and fire with sin and Satan: peace with holiness implies a conflict with, and a victory over, every form of evil. To man's higher and better nature the Lord brought peace; to his lower nature, which is "earthly, sensual, devilish" (S. James iii. 15), He was the herald of war. The doctrine of Jesus Christ is a sword; it is the operating knife in the hand of Him the Great Physician. The functions of a sword are performed by His teaching or doctrine, which :—

I. *Wounds.*—When the body is smitten with a sword it cannot but wound; the blow may not be a hard one, but it must produce some effect. "The sword of teaching" wounds—1) The conscience, by the conviction of sin. It brings home to the conscience its sad and many defalcations; how untrue it has been to itself, and to its better yearnings and promptings. Conscience may have felt a misgiving before: the doctrine of Jesus Christ; His love, power, pardon, and kingdom of grace, wound it to the very quick. 2) The heart or affections, which had been hardened by neglect, by unrepented sin, by a low and sordid view of life. "The sword of teaching" breaks through this outer crust of worldliness, and renders it fit to receive and profit by the dew of Divine grace. 3) The understanding, so long darkened by ignorance of Divine things; a wound or rent is made in it, and the light of the glory of God shines in upon it.

II. *Separates or divides.*—The sword cuts off one member from the rest: a joint or a limb, as the case may be. The "sword of teaching" wielded by Jesus Christ divides—1) The flesh from the spirit; man's lower from his higher nature; the "old man" (Eph. iv. 22) from the "new man;" severing the desires and inclinations of earth from those of heaven. 2) The occasions of sin and temptation. From those who seek to lead a holy life "the sword of teaching" cuts off from evil companions, looks, the indulgence of sinful thoughts. 3) The past life of sin, from the present life of grace and amendment.

III. *Kills.*—The sword sometimes kills; so does the sword of the Lord's teaching. It kills the whole body of indwelling sin, that man should not henceforth serve sin. It slays—1) The life of sin, making man "dead unto sin;" thus checking and staying its further growth and desire. 2) The power of sin. Sin was strong as Goliath before his fall; with its life, the power of sin is destroyed, it can no longer lead man captive at its will. 3) The effects of sin, sorrow, and vanity here; hell and eternal separation from God hereafter.

Epilogue.—Quench not this "Sword of the Spirit, which is the Word of God." (Eph. vi. 17.) Pray and seek that it may perform its work upon your heart—1) Thoroughly; since it is powerful. (Heb. iv. 12.) 2) Savingly; that sin being wounded, separated, and killed within you, the kingdom of heaven may be gained by the violence of the "sword of teaching."

SERMON XV.

GUILTY WORDS.

" By thy words thou shalt be condemned."— *S. Matt.* xii. 37.

Origen.—"Let us therefore take away abominations out of the mouth, removing slanders, words vain, idle, and about to bring accusation against us in the Day of Judgment."—*In Jerem. Homil.* v. *Huet.* vol. i. p. 82, D.

Reflecting upon the words spoken during a single day even, it seems impossible that any one can escape condemnation. Think upon the infinite number of words which have been uttered during a long life. How few of profit; how many of sin. What a mighty effect for everlasting weal or woe have many of our words had. They live long after we are dead and gone; live on in the minds, principles, and actions of those who come after us. With our Blessed Lord's fearful statement before us, we should almost fear to speak at all. Like one of old, we should almost desire to pass our days in silence. Yet the gift of speech was given to us for our use; for justification, and not for condemnation. Out of the almost infinite variety which speech assumes, it is difficult to classify our guilty words which may condemn us. We take then the three classes which a great Father of the Church has set before us; not as being exhaustive, but as being simple, and as leading to an easy personal application. We note—

I. *Thoughtless words.*—Such are the product of an idle and unthinking mind. Any harm which they may do—and they often do a great deal of harm—is not intentional. They proceed from carelessly allowing the mind to ramble on how and whither it will, and the speech to express these ramblings all unheeded and unchecked. They are guilty, not perhaps in what they mean, but from the source whence they spring. Guilty, since they imply a mind which is—1) Undisciplined; having never been properly subjected to God's will and the teaching of conscience. 2) Idle; for we have been too careless to take any thought what the mind shall speak; indifferent as to what its produce may turn out to be. 3) Weak; and so have allowed thought to expend itself recklessly, so that all its strength and self-containment has been lost. Life, with all its earnest purposes; eternity, with its momentous consequences looming in the distance; the mind, with its powers and capacities; the soul, with God's

Spirit ever pleading with it; all rise up to condemn thoughtless words.

II. *Vain words.*—These are more directly guilty than the former class. They imply thought which is directed to a wrong end; the prostitution, by a deliberate intention of the will, of that which God intended to be so great an instrument of good. Vain words lure on to sin; harden the heart; fix the affections upon this lower world; end in disappointment, sorrow, and shame. Vain words are—1) Unholy; they contain no love or reverence for God. 2) Harmful; as leading to neither the purity of the affections nor the cultivation of the understanding. 3) Contemptible; as being below the utterance of a creature made in the image of God the Father, and redeemed by the Precious Blood of God the Son.

III. *Slanderous words.*—Such words are more deadly than the cruellest sword; they slay the reputation of the innocent; they impute wrong motives; they prevent justice; they destroy the mutual love between man and man. Slanderous words are—1) Deadly in their issue; 2) devilish in their origin; 3) degrading in their utterance.

Epilogue.—1) Take as much account of speech as of action. That which you would be ashamed to do, be ashamed to speak of. 2) Pray that your every word may be watched and discreet, so that you "offend not with the tongue." The end of speech is mutual improvement, sympathy and help in things lovely and of good report. See that you receive not this great gift of God in vain.

SERMON XVI.
THE ESTATE OF MAN.

"Thou hast made him a little lower than the Angels, and hast crowned him with glory and honour."—*Ps.* viii. 5.

Origen.—"I say that man is endowed with freedom of will, and, saying this, that he has been exceedingly graced by God. All other things, by a certain necessity, are obedient to the Divine ordination. If you mention heaven, it stands still, bearing rule, not being moved from its defined place. If you desire to speak to me concerning the sun, this perfects its ordained motion, not wandering from its course, but by a certain necessity serving the Lord. And you see the earth truly stable and producing its appointed fruits. Likewise the rest of created things serve their Creator by necessity, nor is any of them able to do anything save that for which they were made. Wherefore we do not praise these things under these conditions obeying their Master; nor for them is there any hope of better things laid up in store, because they have faithfully guarded their decreed state. But

God wills that man should obey with the understanding, and he received the power of governing himself, neither being bound by any necessity of nature nor being deprived of power; so that I say, on account of better things, he is endowed with free will, in order that he may receive more of them from the Better One (which things flow to Him from obedience), and as being a debt from the Creator. I do not say that man is so constituted for his loss, but for his gain. If he had been as one of the elements or their like, a compulsion would have been laid upon him to serve God, yet he would have received no reward worthy of his choice, but man is as an instrument of the Creator, and the cause of those things that he uses. But man would have known nothing better, had he known nothing save that which came to him from nature. Therefore I say that God so honoured man that he should excel in the counsel and in the knowledge of the highest things, and He gave the power to him of doing that which he desired."—*Cont. Mar. sec.* iv. *Wetst.* pp. 103, 104.

The estate of man is indeed but "a little lower than the Angels;" since man was created for earth and not for heaven; and, unlike them, was made subject to certain conditions of time and space; "crowned with glory and honour" as being a creature of a moral order; the recipient of vast powers; the subject of a course of probation; bearing about in his person the image and likeness of God; being God's Vice-regent in the world, and the Lord of all the inferior creatures. The estate of man is one of exceeding dignity, and, alas! one of peril too; a temporary and contingent estate, now at this present time; but one which will quickly pass onwards, either to eternal glorification or to "everlasting shame and contempt." Of this estate of man we note that it is—

I. *Exalted.*—"God so honoured man that he should excel in counsel and in the knowledge of the higher things." Man is infinitely exalted in the possession—1) Of a mind and understanding which differs but in degree from the mind of God Himself; an understanding that by memory connects the past with the present; and from this combined knowledge he can, under certain restrictions, look onwards to the future. (Note a very powerful poem by Byrd, 1588, entitled, "My Mind to me a Kingdom is.") 2) Of a power and dominion. "Thou hast put all things in subjection under his feet." (Ps. viii. 5.) The dominion of man over nature is one great proof of his exalted nature. Man compels the elements even to do his bidding; turning wind, water, and fire into his servants. 3) Of the promise of a future state of absolute perfection, glory, and happiness, as being the heir presumptive to an eternal kingdom. This promised future sanctifies and ennobles the present; removes from sorrow and death all their bitterness and their sting.

II. *Free.*—In possessing freedom of the will man stands above the heaven, the sun, the earth, and the rest of created things. Man is a creature of understanding, will, and feeling, and not of necessity. Man has "received the power of governing himself," and the conditions of such self-government are also within his power. Man is free in—1) Thought and imagination; hence the beautiful conceptions to which the human mind has given birth; no limit to the range of the imaginative and the speculative faculties. 2) Will, purpose, or intent. He can "set himself" in any way that he lists towards heaven or hell; towards glory or abasement. 3) Action; to a large extent to do or to leave undone; to work well or ill during his day of life. When so vast issues hang upon the stake, this freedom of man is indeed a solemn and responsible prerogative.

III. *Progressive.*—The cell of the bee, the web of the spider, the nest of the bird, are all formed now as they were at the beginning; man alone is ever

The Estate of Man. 77

improving; ever going on to that which is higher and better. Knowledge of every kind—art, civilization, etc.—is ever on the increase. One generation begins where the former generation left off. Dare we say that human progress is unlimited? We may say that it is—1) Constant; never leaving off; changing it may be its centres, but ever gaining ground. 2) Contingent upon man's knowledge of and obedience to the laws of God. 3) Tending towards, but never reaching perfection in any one single thing, be it great or small.

IV. *Retributive.*—Neither praise nor reward waits upon compulsory service. Man alone has the hope and the promise that one day " he may receive better things from the Better One." This retribution will be—1) Just; rendered to every man according to his work. 2) Full and ample; no stint with God. 3) Suitable; a reaping as the sowing hath been.

Epilogue.—A personal question: Am I vindicating this my high estate? Is my daily life crowning me with glory and honour?

SERMON XVII.

FELLOW-WORKERS WITH GOD.

"Workers together with Him."—2 *Cor.* vi. 1.

Origen.—" They will be the feet of Christ who run to peace-making; who hasten to help those who are placed in necessity. They will be the hands of Christ which are extended in mercy, which bear help to the needy, which are stretched out as an aid to the weak. So will they also be the eyes of Christ which supply the light of knowledge to another body. (S. Matt. vi. 22.) The teeth, they who are able with the teeth to chew the strong and solid food of the Word of God, and to reduce it to the utmost fineness; those of whom the Apostle speaks in the Epistle to the Hebrews. (Heb. v. 14.) But to the imperfect Corinthians he says, 'I have fed you with milk,' etc. (1 Cor. iii. 2.)"—*In Gen. Hom.* xvii. *Geneb.* vol. i. p. 34, I. K.

The work of Jesus Christ on earth did not cease at His Ascension, but it has been carried on by His faithful servants and followers from that time until now, and it will be continued in the world until the end of time. Blessed are they who are called to have any part or lot in this glorious work which is carried on—

I. *In the Church.*—By duly qualified and rightly ordained persons, unto whom it is committed to administer the Sacraments, and to officiate at public prayer, and to preach, etc. This work of Christ in the Church is perpetuated by a priesthood which is solemnly consecrated to this most holy duty and service. Which act of consecration—1) Conveys the gift of Divine grace which flows through Christ's minister who is duly ordained, as through a channel to those for and to whom he ministers. As the work of Jesus on earth was a work of supernatural grace, so is the work of those who are duly constituted to minister in His Name, to consecrate, to absolve, to baptize, to preach, and to teach. The Kingdom of God must soon come to an end if Orders lost their Divine grace, and the priests of Jesus had only such power and grace as belong to all good Christian people in common. 2) Again, this solemn consecration to the priesthood in a certain degree separates the ordained one from the ordinary and common business of every-day life. It lifts him above the arena of many of the world's struggles, ambitions, disappointments, and successes. It enforces upon him a holier and a calmer life. 3) It ensures, as far as man can ensure anything, that a certain preparation, fitness, and training has preceded the solemn act of ordination; a preparation which, however unworthy its recipient may prove himself hereafter to be, must leave some traces of its good effect upon him which can never wholly pass away. The ordained hands used to consecrate; the mouth used to absolve, bless, reprove, and expound; the eyes used to enlighten darkened souls in the mysteries of the kingdom of heaven; the feet which are swift to carry the message of the Gospel to the ends of the world, may all be truly said to be the hands, eyes, mouth, and feet of Jesus Christ.

II. *In the world.*—This work of Jesus Christ is carried on by means of—1) Schools and colleges "of sound learning and religious instruction," in which Holy Scripture is studied in its original tongues; the history of the Church read from its very beginning; the writings of the great fathers and doctors unearthed, re-edited, and brought to bear upon doctrinal questions. 2) Institutions for healing, reformation, and refuge and help; by means of which the great precepts of the love of Jesus are carried out into their practical workings. 3) Missionary and other enterprises, by which the knowledge of the Person and Kingdom of Jesus is carried into all lands. The missioner goes with swiftness, representing the feet of Jesus Christ; with hands like His extended in loving help; with the voice of Jesus to proclaim the glories of His Gospel; with the eyes of Christ to enlighten the nations which have long walked in darkness. In whatsoever way men work for Jesus in the world, they become His feet, hands, eyes, teeth, as the case may be.

III. *In the heart.*—If the afflictions of Christ can be filled up in the body (Col. i. 24), how much rather can the work of Jesus be wrought out in the soul? The feet of the soul—the thoughts—being swift to travel towards Him; the hands of the mind—the will—extending themselves to receive Him; the eyes of the soul—the understanding—enlightening all the dark recesses of the mind; the teeth of meditation reducing things spiritual to that state in which they can afford nourishment to the inward man.

Epilogue.—The true member of the Body of Christ is a co-worker with Him; all his parts and faculties being devoted to His interest and service. The work of Jesus in this world consists of three spheres of labour: the honour and glory which is due unto His Name and worship; the salvation of the soul, and the bringing it into a state of righteousness through Jesus Christ our Lord; and, lastly, through love to Jesus the seeking in every way to ameliorate man's condition and to aid in the bettering of his estate. To carry on this work, all the members of the body—feet, hands, eyes, etc.—must be pressed into this holy and glorious service.

SERMON XVIII.

THE TABERNACLES OF KNOWLEDGE.

" How goodly are thy tabernacles, O Israel."—*Num.* xxiv. 5.

Origen.—" Tabernacles are the particular dwellings of those who are ever on the road, and are ever walking, and have not found the end of their journey. Israel represents those who display a desire for wisdom and knowledge; of which there is no end. For what will be the limit of the wisdom of God? Where by how much more any one may have approached, by so much more will he find deeper things; and by how much more he may have searched, by so much more will he discover things more ineffable and incomprehensible; for the wisdom of God is incomprehensible and inestimable. Therefore those who make the journey of the wisdom of God are fond of tabernacles, in which they ever walk and ever advance; and the more they advance, by so much is the way of advancing increased for them, and is stretched out towards the immeasurable. And if any one has made some advances in knowledge, and has gained something by experience in such things, he knows truly that when he has lighted upon any theory or agnition of spiritual mysteries, that there the mind tarries as in a certain tabernacle. When, indeed, from those things which it has found, the understanding searches after and advances towards others, then as if the tabernacle was being struck, it reaches forward to higher things, and there it places the seat of the mind, fixed by the stability of the senses; and thence again from these it finds other spiritual senses, which the consequences of the former senses without doubt have disclosed. So the soul ever extending itself to that which is better, seems to walk in certain tabernacles. For the soul when enkindled by the ember of knowledge can never rest and be still, but is ever called forth from good things to better, and again from the better to the highest things."—*In Numb. Hom.* xvii. *Geneb.* vol. i. p. 150, H. I.

It is thus that they—the true and spiritual Israel of God—the holy souls, who being led by the Spirit of God become at length Sons of God (Rom. viii. 14), are ever constrained to press onwards towards the prize of their "high calling of God." (Phil. iii. 14.)

As the spirit, during this life, dwells not in the permanent house, but in the tabernacle of the flesh, so does the mind in its present imperfect state—whilst it sees through a glass darkly—dwell in the tabernacles of Divine love and knowledge, making a continuous and steady progress towards that perfection to which it will one day attain. What similitude more apt could be found to express the highest knowledge of Divine things which can be obtained in this imperfect state in which we only "know in part"? (1 Cor. xiii. 9.) The tent, tabernacle, or dwelling is—

I. *Of slight value.*—Houses or mansions are built of solid material, and are often decorated at a great cost. Tabernacles, on the other hand, are constructed of very simple materials; canvas, cordage, and a few beams and pegs constitute the whole of the structure. So is our present knowledge, compared with that which it will be hereafter, of very slight value; rude and rough, lacking both form and decoration. It is permitted to man to pick up a fragment only of universal knowledge here and there. The finished structure of the temple of knowledge will be built in a perfect place by perfect natures, to endure for a perfect and an eternal state. The canvas of opinion, the cords of love, the pegs of hope, and the beams of labour; these form the tabernacles of knowledge here below, which will be changed into a temple when "we shall know even as we are known." Slight and valueless is our present knowledge as contrasted with its future extension; hence we learn to be—1) Diffident in opinion. 2) Humble in thought. 3) Careful to store up and acquire.

II. *Temporary.*—The tabernacle serves for a purpose and for a time; useful as far as it goes, yet is destined to give place to something higher, better, more worthy and permanent. Our present knowledge, even of Divine things, is fitted for our present imperfect state. There are many revelations which the Lord will one day make to us, but we "cannot bear them now." In this our state of childhood it behoves us to rest content with the rudiments of things. Learn not to confound things temporal and eternal; that eternal knowledge which shall remain for ever, with the fleeting speculations and philosophies of men, which after having had their day, pass away as if they had never been.

III. *Shifting.*—As the march progresses, so does the tabernacle keep pace with it; ever being pitched and ever taken down again. The earnest soul is not content to dwell in one place, but is ever pressing onwards and upwards; striving after the unattained; praying and thirsting for larger and still larger measures of grace and illumination; perpetually moving the tabernacle of knowledge into richer and richer pastures; seeking to penetrate deeper and deeper into the understanding of the Divine mind.

Epilogue.—Led by faith, disciplined by holiness, conformed by love to Jesus Christ, let the soul dwell now in the tabernacle of Divine knowledge; journeying onwards toward that everlasting temple, in which is stored up the fulness of knowledge.

SERMON XIX.
STUMBLINGBLOCKS.

"Woe to that man by whom the offence cometh."—
S. Matt. xviii. 7.

Origen—" But do not believe that there are in nature and in the constitution of things those offences which certain men, through whom they originate, seek out. For as God did not create death, so neither did He beget an offence;—but He begat the freedom of the will, an offence in some not willing to endure hardship for the sake of virtue."—*Comm. in Matt. Huet.* vol. i. p. 328, D. E.

Infinite are the causes of stumbling to a holy life; offences or stumblingblocks are continually rising up on all sides to stay the course of the soul in the knowledge of Divine things; to weaken love; to destroy faith; and to hinder the carrying out into word and deed of many a holy desire and a good resolution. Hence the complaint of the faithful, as to the large amount of evil that there is in the world; of the exceeding sinfulness which attaches itself to all things belonging to this time and life. Whence come these offences, stumblingblocks, or causes of sin? since " it must needs be that offences come." (S. Matt. xviii. 7.) They can but proceed either from God Himself; that is, from the constitution of things as ordered by Him; or from man as turning from holiness to sin; from God to Satan; from man denying his true race and parentage; rejecting his first lawful Master; forfeiting his high estate and privileges of grace. "Man fabricates the sword which stabs his peace" with God; with his fellow man; with his own conscience; which destroys his happiness in this present world, and the certain hope and expectation of happiness in the next. The offence and stumblingblock relates to—

I. *God.*—It is an offence to God when men—1) Distrust His providence. In many ways this is done: Every murmur against God's ordering of the course of life implies a certain amount of distrust, as does every unholy attempt to alter by human strength the course of the Divine will. The unresigned soul is ever distrustful of God's fatherly goodness. Undue taking "thought for the morrow," is another form of the same offence, since it places man's own care, forethought, and action above the workings of the Creator of the world and man. To a noble spirit, nothing is so galling as distrust. With what infinite contempt must the All-wise and All-powerful One view the ungrateful distrust of those creatures who live, move, and have their being in him. 2) Doubt of His Revelation. This is almost a greater offence than the other, since it pertains to the understanding rather than to the affections and the needs of this present life. By such doubt the mind of man sets itself in judgment upon the mind of God; revealing thereby a littleness, combined with a pride and arrogance of intellect with which God must be highly displeased. Such doubt is an expression of that intellectual pride which cast Lucifer (Isa. xiv. 12) from heaven.

II. *Self.*—Man is capable of placing various stumblingblocks in the way of his advance in life, whether it be an outward, moral, or a spiritual advance. Every bad habit, idleness, carelessness, ill-temper, etc., are so many obstacles to success in life; and such bad habits can by proper discipline be first weakened and then destroyed. In the spiritual life offences are occasioned—1) By allowing sinful desires to arise unhindered, and to find a place in the soul. The mind has the power to say, " Get thee behind me, Satan;" and if it does not rebuke, but encourages these messengers from hell, then must the existence and presence of these stumblingblocks be laid to a man's own charge. " Resist the devil (evil desires), and he will flee from you." (S. Jam. iv. 7.) 2) More terrible still, is the offence which is caused by the wilful and habitual indulgence in sin, either of thought, or word, or deed. Such indulgence places a barrier upon the King's highway of the Holy Cross, shutting out all view of the heavenly country; staying all further progress; paralyzing the will, so that it can make no serious endeavour to overcome the stumblingblock, and thus to continue on the heavenly journey. 3) Delay in repentance is an offence which the soul commits against itself, sometimes to its eternal loss. Now, there is time, means, and opportunity to escape from the past, to press onward to higher and holier things, to obtain pardon for that which has gone by, and fresh supplies of grace for that which is to come. How long dare any one say that this season will last?

III. *Others.*—How often does it happen that instead of becoming a help and a blessing, we become a curse and a hindrance to others? The prosperity of the wicked; the seemingly happy life of those altogether unmindful of their souls; the sorrows and afflictions which the righteous are often called upon to bear, all become offences to others who do not view these things aright. Man not seldom becomes an offence to his fellows by his—1) Words, written or spoken; the former a heritage influencing future generations either for evil or for good. 2) Example. The power of example is so great that it is next to impossible to overrate it. Example acts upon others

—*a*) Unconsciously. *b*) Gradually. *c*) Surely ; forming in others, if not a perfect, a partial likeness. How careful should men be to let their "light shine before men."

Epilogue.—Seek in all things to be "void of offence" (Acts xxiv. 16) towards God, others, and yourself. Watch and pray, lest ye enter into this temptation. May the Lord's words ever be sounding in your ears : "Woe unto that man by whom the offence cometh."

SERMON XX.

THE ALTAR OF THE HEART.

" We have an altar."—*Heb.* xiii. 10.

Origen.—" In this building of the church there ought to be also an altar; whence I deem that whosoever of you ' as lively stones are built up ' (1 S. Pet. ii. 5). into it, are ready to be intent upon prayers, and that they may offer ' prayers night and day ' (1 Tim. v. 5,) and sacrifice the victims of supplication. These are they of whom Joshua builds an altar. But note what praises he ascribes to the stones themselves of the altar: ' Joshua built an altar unto the Lord God of Israel, of whole stones over which no man hath lift up any iron.' (Joshua viii. 30, 31.) Who do you imagine are these ' whole stones ?' The conscience of each one knows who is whole and who is uncorrupt, unpolluted, unspotted in the flesh and in the spirit. Who is he ' over which no man hath lift up any iron ?' He who hath not received the darts kindled by an evil concupiscence, but who hath extinguished and repelled them with the shield of faith. It is he who hath never received the iron of contention, of war, of strife; but who hath been ever peaceful, ever quiet and meek, and conformed to the humility of Christ. These are therefore the 'living stones,' out of which our Lord Jesus 'built an altar of whole stones over which no man hath lift up any iron,' that He may offer upon them the burnt offerings and peace offerings."—*In Jesu Nave. Hom.* ix. *Geneb.* i. p. 188, H.

The entire life of man ought to be one long-continued sacrifice of self. That this sacrifice be acceptable to God; that He may bless our endeavours when weak; our discipline of the affections when strong; our conflicts with sin when severe; our offerings of self upon the several shrines of duty, obedience, and love; the motive in all that we do must be holy, pure, and good. In other words, our every thought, word, and deed must upon the altar of the heart be offered as a sacrifice to the God and Father of us all. In order that the sacrifice be acceptable the heart must be—

I. *Entire.*—Composed of "whole stones." It is an attribute of our imperfect nature to allow itself to be divided, mutilated, and so impaired, as to be unable to bring all its powers to a focus; to fix them plainly and consistently upon one object. When the heart is weakened by division, when the altar is built of broken stones, it loses all firm purpose; it will bear the weight upon it of no sacrifices. The "Altar of the heart" must be whole and entire in—1) Desire. Not doing one thing and longing to do another; not walking along the narrow path it may be, but ever and anon casting many a lingering, longing glance towards the other fatal, though more pleasant, road. Conflict of desire deprives the soul of all real rest and calm; it eats out any joy or satisfaction which might follow the commission of a righteous act; it makes the commands of love to be irksome, the burden of duty all but intolerable to bear. Let the desire be whole, and the altar becomes capable of consecrating any sacrifice. 2) Purpose and endeavour. Setting one aim and one object steadily and persistently before it; and using every means and every power to carry it out faithfully, honestly, truly, so far as it is possible to do so. Desire is the fount of endeavour; but without the struggle to obtain, the longing is in vain. 3) Allegiance to the Lord. It is His sacrifice, and only His, which is to be offered upon the "Altar of the heart," not that of the world, the flesh, or the devil; a sacrifice offered through love to Him, in His Name, and for His sake; by Him to be presented through His mediation to the Eternal Father.

II. *Living.*—Composed of "lively stones," (1 S.

Pet. ii. 5.) This altar of the heart must be composed of stones which are not only entire, but which are also instinct with a life which is—1) Glorious: as being glorified by the indwelling Presence of the Holy Ghost, the Lord and Giver of life and glory. 2) Free: delivered from the bondage of sin, and translated into the glorious liberty of the children of God. Free from the obstructions of the whole body of the flesh; liberated from the demands and dominion of our old unregenerated nature. 3) Prophetic: in its yearnings, desires, and aspirations after the infinite and sublime. Prophetic of that life which shall be lived wholly unto God.

III. *Feeling.*—Endowed with an active sensibility to many a pang and many a throe; endued with almost infinite capacities of—1) Sorrow for sin. 2) Joy in repentance and pardon. 3) Hope and trust in the love and mercy of Jesus.

IV. *Deathless.*—Never to pass into nothingness and non-existence; but to be a means by which an eternal sacrifice can be offered to the Father throughout eternity. The power of an endless life must rest upon both altar and sacrifice alike. Deathless, in suffering every kind of change without distinction.

V. *Childlike.*—The Sacred and Immaculate Heart of Jesus was a living Altar, upon which He, whilst He was on earth, offered to His Heavenly Father one

The Altar of the Heart.

continuous sacrifice of the—1) Will. "Not My will but Thine be done." 2) Affections. "Whosoever will do," etc., "the same is my brother and sister and mother." 3) Life. "Father, into Thy hands I commend My spirit." The whole earthly life of Jesus was one unbroken offering of Himself unto the Father upon the Altar of His heart.

Epilogue.—Offered upon such an altar—1) Our meanest sacrifices will be accepted; 2) our commonest gifts will be allowed; 3) our ablest ministrations ever accepted.

SERMON XXI.

HELL.

"Walk in the light of your fire, and in the sparks that ye have kindled."—*Isa.* 1. 11.

Introduction.—" In these words it seems to be pointed out that the sinner kindles for himself the flame of his own fire, and that he will be submerged not in any fire which had been previously kindled by another, or which had existed before himself. The food and material of this fire are our sins, which by the Apostle Paul are named, ' wood, hay, stubble. ' (1 Cor. iii. 12.) I deem also that as a superabundance of meat and food of a given quantity and quality generates fevers in the body of different kinds and durations; so in the soul, when it may have congregated a multitude and abundance of evil works and sins in itself, in due time this entire congregation of sins ferments, and the punishment is inflamed to torments. The conscience itself is agitated and pierced by its particular stings, and becomes an accuser and a witness against itself. (Rom. ii. 15. 16.) From which it can be understood, that from the harmful affections of sins, certain torments are generated around the substance itself of the soul; as when it is wasted by the fires of envy or jealousy; or agitated by the madness of anger; or consumed by the immensity of sadness.

"The 'outer darkness' (S. Matt. xxv. 30) I do not think is to be understood of any atmosphere which is dense and deprived of light, but rather of that darkness of profound ignorance into which they are plunged who are without the light of the Divine understanding."—*Peri Archon.* II. c. xi. *Geneb.* vol. i. pp. 447, E; 448, I.

It may perhaps be lawful when taking a purely subjective view of the question to interpret the expressions of Holy Scripture as to the punishment of the future state somewhat figuratively, and we can then resolve them into the worm of conscience; the fire of sin; and the darkness of ignorance. The Prophet's words are capable of being accommodated in an ironical sense to the wicked and their punishment. Taking the spiritual or subjective view of Hell, we note that it is—

I. *A State, not a Place.*—It is quite possible to be happy and contented in the most miserable of places. With an inward contentment, outward circumstances lose much of their power. It is equally possible to be most miserable amidst all the grandeur, comforts, and refinements of life. Happiness and misery are states, not places. It is a very common mistake to confound place with state; whereas the one may change whilst the other remains permanent; the one may depend upon conditions without a man; the other resting upon that which is in his own power.

II. *A state of our own making.*—By means of sin we can make a hell for ourselves; by a right use of Divine grace we can make a heaven. God has given us great power and means, whereby we can order ourselves either for happiness or for misery. The formation of a spiritual hell is a mighty abuse of man's prerogative of free will; such formation being the result of the will's—1) consent to; 2) preference for; 3) persistence in sin.

III. *A state which is present with us now.*—We need not wait to enter into this spiritual hell until we die. Many and many a soul who is now living on earth is truly living in hell. The worm of a remorseful conscience is ever gnawing; the fire of sinful thoughts, lust, anger, envy, revenge, is ever burning, consuming the noblest qualities of the soul. In the "outer darkness" of despair are quenched all the hopes, desires, affections, and aspirations which make a man Godlike, and which prepare him for heaven. The hell on earth is the beginning of a more fearful hell to be entered upon after death.

IV. *A state from which there is only one deliverance.*—The sinner, now burning in the pains of his spiritual hell, calls out in an agony, "O wretched man that I am! Who shall deliver me from the body of this death?" (Rom. vii. 24.) Who? Only One can do so. He Who came to deliver out of the hands of Satan those whom he held in such dire bondage. Jesus Christ can deliver you. He can pardon you and save you: quench your fire in His living water of grace; your sparks in the ocean of His love.

Epilogue.—Now before the second death cometh upon you, O sinner, call upon your Saviour; come out of this spiritual hell, and then hereafter you will be delivered from that hell which is both a state and a place.

SERMON XXII.

HOLY PERSUASION.

"We persuade men."—2 *Cor.* v. 11.

Origen.—"Not only is energy needed in him persuading, but also complaisantness on the part of him who is persuaded—the acceptance of the things spoken by the persuader. It is no fault of God if He does not persuade, but of those who do not receive the precious words of God. Eloquence moves some, but does not affect others. Although persuasive words proceed from God belief does not come from Him, as S. Paul plainly teaches us in these words, 'This persuasion cometh not of Him that calleth you.' (Gal. v. 8.) Such also is the passage, 'If ye be willing and obedient,' etc. (Isa. 1. 19, 20.) For as some one may desire those things of which the minister speaks, and obeying, becomes worthy of the promise of God, there is need of the assent and purpose of the hearer, as it is solemnly declared in Deuteronomy, 'What doth the Lord thy God require of thee, but to fear the Lord,'" etc.—(Deut. x. 12, 13.)—*C. Celsum.* lib. vi. c. lvii.

Stern as was our Blessed Lord in denouncing every form of sin, secret as well as open; plain and uncompromising as were all His statements as to the obedience, self-denial, love, and other Christian graces by which the kingdom of heaven was to be gained; still persuasion formed the groundwork of His teaching and ministration to men. Persuasion was the main factor in those " cords of a man and bands of love" (Hosea xi. 4) by which He drew such multitudes of hearts to Himself. In His words are to be found persuasive invitations (S. Matt. xi. 28), persuasive parables, persuasive promises. His many "mighty works" invited men to love and to follow Him; persuaded them of His love for their bodies as well as their souls. Jesus Christ might well have said that which the Apostle said long afterwards, "We persuade men." The Lord could, had He willed it, have compelled men to accept His Divine message; He rather persuaded them, since He knew that persuasion was far better than compulsion, inasmuch as it is—

I. *Kind and gentle.*—Harshness and bitterness were alien from the mind and purpose of Jesus, when to seek and to save the lost, He visited in love and mercy this sin-ridden and sorrow-stricken world.

The Mission and Gospel of Jesus Christ did not appeal to craven fear, or to sordid terror, but it did and does appeal to the higher faculties of—1) Conviction; by which the whole profitlessness and mistake of an unholy life is made clear to the conscience. 2) Compunction; by which is engendered an intense sorrow that so many past sins of omission and commission should lie at the door of the soul; sure evidences of an ungrateful, careless, and hard heart. 3) Love; by which a complete purification and pardon should be assured to the offender. It was because the Lord appealed ever to the higher, rather than to the lower, faculties of our race that He used, in His dealings with men, persuasion rather than compulsion, and thus made it allowable for the Apostles to beseech "by the meekness and gentleness of Christ." —2 Cor. x. 1.

II. *Liberal.*—Persuasion, unlike force of any kind, recognizes the higher elements of our nature. It addresses man as a being possessed of—1) Reason. Hence the Lord often discoursed and argued with men; and promised moreover that after His departure from the world the appeal to reason should not cease. (S. John xvi. 8.) Persuasion implies a relationship between man's state and his faculties; between his present and his future. 2) Freedom of will; either to accept or to reject that which is offered. Without freedom of will, persuasion would be used in vain, there would be no qualities upon which it could act. It would lead to nothing. 3) Conscience; which passes an approving or disapproving sentence upon every thought, word, or deed. Persuasion is fully adapted to natures which were created after the likeness and in the image of God.

III. *Thorough.*—A reaching down to the depths of man's moral and spiritual being. Compulsion is but superficial; it can command an outward service only; it leaves the depths of the soul untouched. Persuasion, as a key, unlocks the nature of the inner man, reaching downwards to the—1) Affections; enlisting them on its side, and inclining the heart to open itself as it directs. 2) Desires; influencing those many yearnings of the soul that hardly find a definite expression in words. 3) Purposes; whence spring those resolutions which it is the special attribute of persuasion to engender. Our Blessed Lord used persuasion in order to reach the inner soul and conscience of man; to melt his hard heart; to subdue his unruly will; to lead him onwards gently, tenderly, and safely to those higher gifts and graces which He had to bestow.

IV. *Powerful.*—Persuasion is all-powerful; it takes possession of and moulds the entire man. It allows of no—1) Opposition; barriers and objections break down before it. 2) Division; all the faculties and powers must work with one will and one mind. 3) Doubt; one by one it dissolves all the clouds and darkness by which the mental vision may be encompassed.

Epilogue.—Hearken unto the voice of Holy persuasion; let it—1) Lead; 2) govern; 3) enlighten thy life. It is a mighty influence for good. Remember the old Æsopian fable of "The Sun and the Wind."

SERMON XXIII.

THE MYSTERY OF PROBATION.

" The Lord your God proveth you, to know whether ye love the Lord your God with all your heart."—*Deut.* xiii. 3.

Origen.—" We must consider the fact, that it was not immediately after the departure from Egypt that the people were numbered. Nor is it said they were numbered, when having passed over the Red Sea they came to the desert. For not yet had they been tempted; nor yet had they been attacked by the enemy. They contended against Amalek and conquered; but not then, indeed, were they numbered; for one victory did not suffice for the perfection of those advancing. They receive the food of manna, and they drink the draught of the water from 'the rock that followed them;' but not then were they numbered; for not yet in them had grown up the things which are said to be fitting for their numbering. The Tabernacle of witness is constructed; but not then even had come the time for numbering the people. The law is given by Moses; the order of the sacrifices is delivered; the rite of purification is taught; the laws of sanctification and the sacraments are instituted; and then by the command of God the people are led to the numbering. Write, O hearer, these words doubly and trebly upon thy heart. See how great are the things which are transferred to thee; how great things are endured; how many advances, how many temptations, how many conflicts there are for you to engage in and conquer, in order that you may be able to be enrolled in the Divine number, that you may be included in some reckoning with God."—*In Numb. Hom.* ii. *Geneb.* vol. i. p. 114, G. H.

The probation of the Israelites was only one more expression of that general law which God has observed in dealing with His creatures ever since man was "created and made." Probation is a law of life, whether it be viewed in relation to the life that now is, or in reference to that which is to come. There is nothing which is worth the having that can be gained without toil, discipline, thought, and some form of self-sacrifice, and the very means employed to gain the desired end, becomes in itself the cause of trial or probation. This is eminently true of the Christian course. It is only after a life of conflict with self, of struggle against sin; of earnest endeavours after holiness; and of a successful issue arising out of all this, that the promise of inheritance (Rev. xxi. 7) passes into a possession. The eternal inheritance and sonship of God depends upon an accepted probation which has been first passed through. Glorious things are written, both to and for "him that overcometh." (Rev. iii. 12.) Yet does man's probation remain, and will remain, to the end of time a mystery. We cannot understand why God, having the power, did not give man grace enough to fulfil all His commands; why He left him with the possibility of "falling away into perdition;" why, in short, He demanded a probation in which man might fail, and thus frustrate both the schemes of nature and of grace in relation to himself. Although understanding it not, we cannot fail to perceive that this mystery of probation is—

I. *Wise.*—It is adapted to the constitution of man. As a creature of free will, endowed with reason, man is rightly subjected to a discipline which will end either in reward or punishment, according to the manner in which it has been used. Wise: inasmuch as it—1) Restrains many an unholy appetite and desire. Sorrow and suffering of all kinds have a purifying influence: softening the heart; lowering the tone of the "animal man;" limiting both the desires and the means for their fulfilment. 2) Strengthens. Body and soul alike are braced by discipline. The very act of nerving up to the resistance of sin or of self, braces and invigorates the moral nature. What exercise in due and proper measure is to the body, and study is to the mind, that is the discipline of probation to the entire life, including body, soul, and spirit. 3) Developes. Great crises bring out great characters; great needs elicit the powers required to meet these needs. God desires to make the best of man, fallen as he is, and therefore He introduces the mystery of probation, which pertains alike to the orders of virtue and of grace.

II. *Consistent.*—It harmonizes with the other attributes and perfections of God. Our Heavenly Father is too merciful and loving either to force His creatures against their will, or to crush them by a blind fate; He is too holy to reward and encourage any infraction of His own laws: God therefore places man in a state of probation; He endows him with supernatural grace, and leaves him a free agent, to be either true or untrue to his high and holy calling. The mystery of probation is thus consistent with God's —1) Mercy; 2) holiness; 3) truth.

III. *Glorious.*—It affords man the prospect and expectation of working out "a far more exceeding and eternal weight of glory;" of rising, through the work and merits of Jesus, to a state of dignity which is beyond that of either angel or archangel. Suffering enhanced the glory and dignity of Jesus. (Phil. ii. 8, 9.) "No cross, no crown;" no conflict, no victory; no endeavour, no means. The mystery of probation is glorious in its—1) Working upon man; exalting, perfecting, purifying him. 2) Preservation of the honour and dignity of God, as connected with man's salvation. 3) Rewards and honours which it promises to those who have " striven lawfully."

Epilogue.—Be true to your heavenly probation. "Work out your own salvation with fear and trembling" (Phil. ii. 12, 13), for God is your fellow-worker; and " endure hardness as a good soldier of Jesus Christ."—2 Tim. ii. 3.

SERMON XXIV.

THE LIGHT OF TRUTH.

"A light that shineth in a dark place."—2 *S. Pet.* i. 19.

Origen.—" If any one desires to search the Divine dogmas of truth, lovingly and not strife-lovingly, he will find the most far-beaming truth."—*Cont. Marc. Wets.*, p. 70.

The common life of man is a state in which the clouds and darkness of error and of doubt are all around him; he wanders first hither and then thither, seeking in vain to find and to follow " the path of life;" he has lost his track; motive, principle, faith, are alike enveloped in the common gloom; he knows not whether to press forwards or to stand still; to rest or to advance; to turn to the right hand or to the left. He cannot see his way before him. Often in the sorest time of doubt or of despair, a light is seen; the " light of truth," following which he walks on his way rejoicing for this light both guides and enlightens him; since it shows—

I. *Surely.*—Truth can neither lie nor deceive. It

cannot be gainsaid or overcome. Truth ever conquers. Hence when our Blessed Lord came down to earth to show to man the way to heaven, He said, "I am the Truth," as well as, "I am the Light of the world;" that if any man should follow Him Who is the Light of Truth he might not walk on in darkness, but should have the light of life. Truth would cease to be truth, could it in anywise deceive or delude. There are many false lights in the world, like that of the "Ignis Fatuus;" but there is only one "light of truth," though it be many-sided and variously coloured in its rays. There are physical truths, moral truths, intellectual truths, spiritual truths; all of which are radiations from the one "light of truth," which emanates from the God of truth. There can be no wrong going in following the light of truth, since all truth is—1) Consistent and harmonious. No one truth can contradict another truth. Anything that admits of a valid contradiction cannot be a real truth. 2) A reflection of the mind of God Who has revealed His nature in His laws and in His Word: in His book of nature as well as in His book of grace. 3) A purifier of the mind, from that darkness of ignorance which is the result of sin and degradation. Truth being so sure a guide can be—1) Implicitly trusted; 2) humbly followed; 3) reverently treated.

II. *Universally.*—The "far-beaming light" of truth

shines—1) Above the world; and is a beacon by which the rocks and shoals of error can be avoided. It becomes a guide by which man is led on to glory. It shines above the world, setting before men an aim; just as the Star of Jesus incited the wise men onward and led them to Bethlehem. 2) On the world; not only as a guide overhead, but as a lamp to our feet and a light to our path; showing the right road to life, and revealing the different turnings and features of that road. Hence truth gives to this world a life and a promise; supplying a means by which men may walk on to higher and better and holier things. 3) In the world; in and among men, being to them both a source of comfort and of strength. Like the sun, truth can be seen by all, felt by all; and like the sun it cheers and invigorates all who bask under its blessed and kindly influence.

III. *Continually.*—Not waning like the inconstant moon, but always appearing, and ever the same, Hence the light of truth never—1) Ages; never grows old. A truth once born into the world can neither age nor die. It is as bright and fresh now as at the moment of its propagation. Truth in the world is the representative of that enduring state in which decay and death are alike unknown. 2) Changes. Men alter the relations under which they may regard truth, but truth itself is changeless. As in passing swiftly through the country the objects are perpetually changing to our view according to our position in relation to them, so men in their travels of life are ever viewing one and the same truth under altered circumstances and connections. 3) Wearies. Its adaptive power is so great, that in one form or another it appeals to the heart with a vigour and a freshness as if heard for the first time. The Holy Gospels are never stale, never tedious; we both read them and listen to them over and over again, year after year, and day after day; and yet they are always bright and fresh to the soul. "Far-beaming truth" has ever shone over this world of darkness and of sin.

IV. *Clearly.*—Every form of error is misty and indistinct; has no clear outline, consequence, or connection. "Far-beaming truth" ever shines with a clear and transparent light, that there may be no possible mistake between it and its counterfeit. Truth is clear in its—1) Statements. It admits of no double meaning. It conceals nothing that ought to be communicated. The lying oracles of Pagan Greece were invested with a twofold sense, so that one way or another the prophecy must be fulfilled. 2) Consequences. The deductions which flow from it are as unequivocal as the parent whence they sprang. (3 Adaptation. Presenting itself to the mind in that due proportion in which each particular understanding is capable of laying hold of it. Hence the "Divine dogmas" are clear to all, although differently comprehended by each one according to his spiritual and intellectual conception. The peasant has a perfectly clear conception of "the truth as it is in Jesus;" though his conception differs materially from the grasp of that same truth by a mind of higher cultivation and of larger powers.

V. *Profitably.*—" Far-beaming truth" does not shine as a dry or a barren light; like the sun, it has to do for the world of men that which the chief luminary of our system does for the world of nature. It—1) Dispels like the sun the mists of darkness, of ignorance, and of error; showing all things in a clear and true light. This mist of error lends the one great enchantment to sin. 2) Reveals fully all defects; shuts out all false reasonings, and condemns all false hopes. 3) Restores and heals many hopeless and fainthearted ones, who have been waiting for further light.

Epilogue.—Man's duty towards truth is urgent and solemn; he is bound to—1) Cherish it; lest any truth be lost to him. 2) Submit himself to it. Truth speaks with a supreme authority. 3) Revere it; so that it be not tampered with by error.

SERMON XXV.

A HOLY MAN.

"He is holy unto his God."— *Levit.* xxi. 7.

Origen.—"If you have understood why an animal, or vessel, or garment is called holy, understand consequently that by these observations and laws man is also called holy. For if any one has consecrated himself to God; if any one shall have implicated himself in no secular concerns, that he may please Him to Whom he has commended himself; if any one has separated and severed himself from the rest of men who are living carnally and bound up in worldly affairs— not seeking the things which are upon earth, but those which are in heaven—such an one is deservedly called holy. For whilst he is mixed up with the crowd, and is enrolled in the multitude of the doubtful, neither is he intent upon God alone, nor is he severed from the herd;—he is not able to be holy."—*In Levit. Hom.* xi. *Geneb.* vol. i. p. 100, H.

The idea of holiness which is contained in these words is one of separation. Separation "unto his

God;" separation from worldly concerns as a matter of pleasure; separation from those who live without God in this world, and for this world alone; separation from the tumults, doubts, and strifes of those who are led hither and thither, ever seeking something that is new. Holiness has been described under other aspects, such as the likeness to, and union with, Jesus Christ; the daily and hourly realization of the heavenly citizenship; the strict discipline or denial of self in such a measure that it becomes the carrying of a daily cross; all of which are other qualifications of the same great Christian grace. At present we will consider the holy man as one who is separated from his unholy fellows, and from the world which is lying around him, by his—

I. *Devotion.*—The holy man "is holy unto his God;" dedicated and consecrated to His honour and service. This devoted separation is—1) Continuous. It was commenced at Baptism, carried on by Confirmation and First Communion, and is sustained by the perpetual and increasing nourishment of the spiritual life. Once broken by a lapse into deadly sin, the continuity of the stream and channel of grace once cut off, it is hard indeed to be regained. The "temple of God" has been defiled, and many tears of contrition and repentance are needed to cleanse it again. It is always easier to destroy, than to create; to pollute, than to cleanse; to deface, than to restore. 2) Entire.

God accepts of no half heart. "Ye cannot serve God and mammon." (S. Matt. vi. 24.) With all the powers of the soul directed to this one object, the service which man can render to God is but feeble and imperfect; and it is only accepted by Him when He can make a gracious allowance for the shortcomings of the soul, knowing in all truth that "she hath done what she could." (S. Matt. xiv. 8.) 3) Voluntary. Most willingly and lovingly rendered devotion, dedication, and service; no fear of hell or hope of heaven being mixed up with it; but simply the love of God, and gratitude to Him constituting the sole cause by which the soul seeks ever more and more to surrender itself up freely, wholly, and continually to Jesus Christ.

II. *Aims and desires.*—The holy man aims not at "the things which are upon earth, but [at] those which are in heaven." His affections and thoughts are associated with things both above and beyond the realm of time and sense. A life and spirit not of nature but of grace has been vouchsafed to him; leading him to despise and soar beyond—1) The passing gratification of the senses. Yet over how many, do the senses of the body exercise a rigorous if unconscious sway. They live to gratify the appetites of the body, even if it be in their less harmful propensities of sight and sound, to say nothing of their grosser and more animal manifestations. 2) The present life and temporal gain of riches, honour, and the like. Worldly advancement, in some one of its many forms, is the one absorbing desire of thousands, nay, of tens of thousands, of redeemed immortal natures, who yet know and feel the shortness of the time during which they are permitted to remain in this world. 3) The natural conceptions and creations of the mind. Faith carries the soul into a region in which reason has no power to follow. The holy soul derives its highest inspirations not from its own imaginings and conceits, but from the strivings and revealings of that Spirit Who takes of the things of God which are spiritually discerned and shows them unto it.

III. *Actions.*—The actions of the holy man are all performed with this one object, " that he may please Him to Whom he has commended himself;" they are therefore not regulated by reference—1) To any code of earthly laws. The world allows of and glories in many deeds which God has forbidden in the most positive manner possible. It pleads for the exercise of revenge and anger; the rendering of evil for evil, which the Saviour emphatically denounced. The " Codex Legum " of man is the expression of a necessary temporizing with human imperfection and crime; whilst that of God aims at the renovation and restitution of his moral and spiritual nature. 2) They are performed without any reference to temporal gain or loss; they have respect "unto the recompence of the reward" in another and holier kingdom, in a higher and nobler condition of being.

Epilogue.—The holy man—1) Is a contradiction of the world by his consecration to God, in his aims, and in his actions. 2) Is a standing protest against its weakness, sorrow, and sin. 3) Is a prophet of a high and solemn order, who, by "his life and doctrine," proclaims that he belongs to another kingdom which is "not of this world;" a kingdom which is eternal, glorious, and happy, because it is holy. His Master's words are for ever ringing in his ears: "Be ye holy, for I am holy."

SERMON XXVI.

THE WINE OF JOY.

"I will not drink henceforth of this fruit of the vine, until that day when I drink it new with you in My Father's kingdom."
—S. *Matt.* xxvi. 29.

Origen.—" We read: 'Thou shalt make them drink of the river of Thy pleasures.' (Ps. xxxvi. 8.) The Lord also says in Jeremiah: 'I will satiate [*inebriabo*] my people.' (Jer. xxxi. 14.) And Isaiah says, 'Behold, My servants shall drink.' (Isa. lxv. 13.) And you will find in Holy Scripture many things related of this same inebriation. Which drunkenness is accepted, without doubt, for joy of soul and rejoicing of mind. If we have, therefore, understood what this drunkenness is, and how it is granted to the holy in promise, we can understand how it is that our Saviour does not drink wine until He shall drink it new in the Kingdom of God. My Saviour also now grieves over my sins. My Saviour cannot be joyful whilst I remain in iniquity. Why not? Because He is the Advocate with the Father on behalf of our sins. (1 S. John ii. 1.) How can He therefore, Who is the Advocate for my sins, drink the wine of joy, He Whom I grieve by sinning? I will drink it, He says, 'with you in my Father's Kingdom.' As long as we so act that we cannot ascend to that kingdom, so long is He, alone, not able to drink that wine which He promised that He would drink with us. He is, therefore, so long in sorrow, as we persist in error."—*In Levit. Hom.* vii. *Geneb.* vol. i. p. 85, A. B.

The fact that man's sin and failing upon earth can affect the state of the Son of God in the glory of Heaven, shows how intimate is the relationship which exists between Jesus Christ and the race which He came to redeem and to exalt; how His wondrous life in eternity is bound up with our dark and erring life in time. The "with you" of the Gospel gives one more view of that close bond of unity which joins the Head to all the members of His mystical body; proving, as it does, that if one of the members suffer, all the members suffer with it. That man can stay or mar the perfect happiness of Jesus; can delay His draught of the "Wine of Joy," is a fresh revelation of the attributes of Jesus Christ towards us of—

I. *Patience.*—His own work for man was quickly

done. He delayed not either His Incarnation, mission, or death, one moment beyond the appointed time. He was ever ready, willing, and waiting to fulfil all His Father's will. It is man, and not God, who delays and procrastinates, and who wastes the precious moments, seasons, and occasions of grace. Jesus was both prompt to act, and is alike patient to wait. His patience in tarrying for the completion of His Kingdom is—1) Inexhaustible in its nature. It outlasts all man's prevarications and delays. There is no time, whilst the season of grace lasts, during which the patience of Jesus can be worn out or exhausted. Had it not been so, long since would He have given up the sons of men to their lost estate and ruin. 2) Untiring in its operation. It was so when He was on earth ; enabling Him to bear with meekness every rebuff, all scorn and contumely. 3) Blessed in its results. Gaining many a soul by His patient waiting for it. Because Jesus is thus patient is it for us to put His patience to a severer test, to tax it to the uttermost of our feeble power? Dare we, as Christians, abuse His goodness by our delayed repentance? He is waiting to drink the "Wine of Joy" with us in heaven.

II. *Sympathy.*—It is not enough for Him by Himself to drink the new wine in His kingdom of glory ; He must drink "with you ;" with our race. The noblest natures upon earth have but small care for solitary pleasures; their joy is but a half gladness when it is not shared with others. The great happiness of heaven will consist in the fact that the joy of one will be the joy of all. With us sympathy is a need, because of the imperfection of our nature; with Jesus it is the expression of a heart overflowing with love, going out towards us not for His sake, but for our own. This sympathy arises from His perfect knowledge of—1) What we are now; so helpless, tied, and bound, so dependent, so weak; so untrue to ourselves in all things, both temporal and spiritual. 2) What we are capable of becoming when all the latent powers of the soul are developed, and the purification shall be made of the incrustations of this lower life. The sympathy of Jesus consists of the two factors, pity and hope. He is longing to drink " the Wine of Joy " with us in heaven.

III. *Condescension.*—" With you;" knowing full well that which you once were; and remembering that it is only by My favour and grace that you are what you are now. " With you;" not with the Father and the Holy Ghost only, nor with the blessed orders of the Angelical or Heavenly Hierarchy only; but " with you," who were once poor degraded outcasts, who by slow degrees have been purified from sin, and admitted into the company of the "just men made perfect." This infinite condescension of Jesus is—1) Of purpose, not of impulse; is a part of the settled order of His Divine grace towards us. When He planned our recovery, it was that He might become the Elder Brother of our race; and the condescension of earth was to be continued and perfected in heaven. 2) Of no degree; unlimited in its operation, there was naturally before the Incarnation no common measure between Jesus and the human race. Now He will never be ashamed to drink " the Wine of Joy " with the redeemed.

Epilogue.—Resolve so to act that you may be found worthy to ascend at length to that kingdom, and to drink the new " Wine of Joy" with Jesus. Resolve not to lengthen His sorrow by your continued sin and impenitence, but rather to present Him with the first fruits of the " Wine of Joy," by your holiness of life.

SERMON XXVII.

THE KNOWLEDGE OF JESUS.

"When the Son of Man shall come in His glory, and all the holy Angels with Him, then shall He sit upon the throne of His glory: and before Him shall be gathered all nations."—*S. Matt.* xxv. 31, 32.

Origen.—"I think that there will be a time of the Advent of Christ in which there will be so great a manifestation of His Person and His Divinity, that not only none of the righteous, but that not one of the sinners will be ignorant of Him as He really is; when also sinners will know their sins in His sight, and the righteous will manifestly see the goal to which their seeds of holiness have brought them. 'And before Him shall be gathered all nations;' they will know Christ as He is."—*In Diversos Hom.* ix. *Geneb.* vol. ii. p. 289, F.

How changed would be the present condition of the world, if throughout its length and breadth there was diffused a just, though even a partial, knowledge of Jesus Christ. How many sins would be prevented;

how many souls would be saved; how greatly would the joy and peace of earth be multiplied. The world would seem like a new place altogether, if the "Person and Divinity" of Jesus were brought home to men's hearts; for then sinners would understand the course of sin, and the righteous would have more certain proof of the end of their life and conversation. Seeking for a perfect knowledge of Him at His coming, we note that the imperfect knowledge which we can gain of Him now is for the practical purposes of life—

I. *Perfect and sufficient.*—Jesus Christ was perfect man, as well as perfect God; and being this, the knowledge of Him brings with it a knowledge of human nature in its fulness and perfection. 1) Jesus was infinitely wise in the understanding, for "in Him dwelleth all the wisdom of the Godhead bodily." (Col. ii. 9.) Knowing this wisdom, we can reach to the heights of the loftiest intelligence. "The mind of Christ" is the most profound and expansive mind that was ever contained in the tabernacle of our flesh. He saw "before and after;" no mistake could be made by Him in anything. Hence, in knowing Him, we know all things. At present, alas, "such knowledge is too wonderful and excellent, for we cannot attain unto it." (Ps. cxxxix. 6.) 2) Jesus was infinitely pure in feeling. His loving heart probed the capacities of our loving nature to its very depth. In knowing Him, we know what true affection means; what unselfish, burning love for others implies. The emotional nature of man is mirrored in its tenderest guise in the sympathetic soul of "the Man of sorrows." 3) Jesus was infinitely holy in action: "This man hath done nothing amiss." (S. Luke xxiii. 41.) The principles of action can be traced in Him to their truest and most exalted source. The knowledge of Jesus must be the basis of all sound knowledge of self; and it brings with it the knowledge of sin in its beginning, course, and end; and the knowledge of holiness in its seed, growth, and development; so that by it "the righteous will manifestly see the goal to which their seeds of holiness have brought them." Hence the knowledge of Jesus Christ is satisfying to the soul: it leaves nothing further to be desired.

II. *Purifying.*—The knowledge of Jesus cannot exist in the soul without its exerting a purifying influence upon the whole man—body, soul, and spirit. It is like "the leaven which leaveneth the whole lump." (1 Co. v. 6.) Knowing Him, the desire to become like Him acquires an irresistible power. It purifies the soul from—1) Worldliness: by the contemplation of His unworldly life. "My kingdom is not of this world." (S. John xviii. 36.) Jesus Christ reversed the world's traditions. 2) Error: "I am the Truth."—S. John xiv. 6.) No one really prefers error to truth; many fall into it, blinded by sin, or as still being surrounded by the mists of ignorance or superstition. If clearly seen truth will ever conquer error. The knowledge of Jesus Christ corrects errors of all kinds : of life, of thought, and of action. 3) Sin: the loving one seeks to be like the beloved. The good cannot be known without a certain desire after the imitation of such goodness being engendered. All true knowledge refines the soul; but the knowledge of Jesus Christ cleanses it in an eminent degree.

III. *Personal.*—Jesus Christ is no mere spiritual or philosophical abstraction; but a living Lord and Saviour : High Priest, Prophet, King, and Elder Brother of our race. In knowing Him we know a Person Who is—1) Infinitely lovely. " Thou art fairer than the children of men. Grace is poured into Thy lips." (Ps. xlv. 2.) Men often, by a most strange contradiction, love all else but Jesus; they love the beautiful in earth, air, water, in men and women, in all creation, save in the Author of creation; Himself being the fairest and most beautiful of all. Yet there cannot be found one dark or ugly spot upon the person of Jesus Christ. 2) Infinitely loving. One Who never turns away from any who come to Him; nay, rather the greater their need, the larger becomes the measure of His love. 3) Infinitely united to and bound up with mankind in time and in eternity. In time, a tender Friend and a mighty Saviour; in eternity, to become the cause of everlasting joy, gratitude, and adoration.

Epilogue.—What is the want which the knowledge of Jesus Christ will not supply? What is the gain of all other knowledge, lacking this? Is there any other knowledge so lasting, so universal, so all-important in its consequences as is this? Does not each question demand an assent? If so, may all men be led to make it their daily prayer, "That I may know Him," etc. (Phil. iii. 10.)

SERMON XXVIII.
IMMORTALITY.

"This is life eternal, that they might know Thee the only true God, and Jesus Christ, Whom Thou hast sent."—*S. John* xvii. 3.

Origen.—" 'I have set before you life and death; therefore choose life.' (Deut. xxx. 19.) If the human race had done this, verily it would never have embraced the mortal condition. But since man leaving life has followed death, this has come to pass. I ask, what is that death which he says 'I have set before you?' Of the life itself it cannot be doubted that God will point out Himself, Who said, 'I am the truth and life.' (S. John xiv. 6.) What is that death, contrary to life, which God has placed before us? I think that it was of it that Paul said, 'The last enemy that shall be destroyed is death.' (1 Cor. xv. 26.) This is therefore the enemy, the devil, who at the first verily was set before us, but is destroyed the last. He has been set before us, not that we should follow, but that we should avoid Him. Whence I consider that the human soul, of itself, cannot be said to be either mortal or immortal ; but that if it should lay hold of life it will be immortal from the participation of life ; but if that, turning itself from life it should contract the beginning of death, it causes itself to become mortal. Therefore the Prophet says, 'The soul that sinneth, it shall die.' (Ezek. xviii. 4.) Although we are of opinion that its death is not the destruction of substance, yet we believe that to be really death which is alien and exile from God Who is the true life."—*In Levit. Hom.* x. *Geneb.* vol. i. p. 98, I. K.

When thoroughly sifted and analysed, our notions of the eternal world beyond the grave are confessedly vague and indistinct. We are so accustomed to use a certain set of words and phrases in reference to the future, that we have become for the most part quite content to rest in them, without pausing to consider whether or not they carry any definite meaning with them. If it be, as most assuredly it is, " life eternal " to know God and Jesus Christ ; that is, to love, serve, and obey them ; to accept the scheme of redemption which is offered to us by the Saviour ; then, by inference, it must be something short of eternal life not to know them. Is there a middle path between eternal death and life? We know of no such. The consideration of the immortality of the soul leads to the conviction that such immortality implies—

I. *A Distinction.*—It is not a paradox to say that there is a life which is truly death; and that there is a death which is truly life. Life, as a state, consists of the due and proper exercise, development, and use of every function and faculty of the living being. Where this takes place, there is perfect holiness, happiness, and content. Nothing further is left to be either longed for or striven after. Life, as a principle, consists of a certain something which, while it is present, keeps death at bay. In some stages of disease, a large portion of the body may be absolutely dead; the state of the patient is a state of death; but whilst that subtle visitant—the principle of life—is there, the body is not dead, it remains still an inhabitant of "the land of the living." This principle of life forms that which this great Father and thinker calls the substance [*substantia*] of the soul. This substance, *ens* or being, can never die; hence it can be subject to an eternal state of death. Could it die, death must happen in a given instant of time, and the soul would pass at once out of existence. It was the purpose and object of Jesus coming into this world, that this principle of life in the soul of man might, by His merits and intercession and pardon, be led to attain to a state of life, that is of perfection and of enjoyment, for ever and ever. These distinctions then, force themselves upon us—1) Both the principle and the state of life in the body can be killed, and itself reduced to non-existence. 2) The state, but not the principle of life in the soul can be killed, yet it cannot be preserved from an eternal state of death. 3) The contrast is most marked between relative values of the principle and the state of life; the latter being of an infinitely higher value.

II. *A Condition.*—If we accept such means as God has placed before us in His infinite mercy and love, the state of "life eternal," in which the substance, *ens* or being, of the soul will be placed for ever in glory, perfection and happiness, will become ours. Reject this grace, degrade, debase, and defile the soul, and then its substance, *ens* or being, will be for ever placed in that state of misery, imperfection, and unfulfilled desire, which is justly spoken of as eternal death. The state of eternal death, or eternal life, is in the power of each Christian sou the principle of life, which must be subject to one or other of these influences, is wholly beyond man's power to affect. The conditions under which the state of eternal life can be obtained are—1) Within man's power. 2) The highest and best under which he can live. 3) The producers of the largest amount of happiness. The question may well be asked, Why, O man, wilt thou elect to enter into the state of eternal death?

III. *A Present.*—The life of the soul is independent of the life of the body, and therefore its state of eternal life can surely begin here on earth. Many elements of the heavenly life can find an exercise and operation before the soul is separated from its present perishable tabernacle of the flesh. The eternal life of the soul has begun, whilst as yet the body has to die. Hence the exercise of holiness, faith, love, and the other Christian graces is the exercise of immortality; and each several act of goodness becomes a factor in the soul's eternal life. Holiness is not a mere obeying of the law of Jesus and walking conformably to His will and mind, but it is the entering into the state of immortality, the glories of which will be fully enjoyed in another and higher state of being. Well may we ask, "O death, where is thy sting?" The resolution should on these grounds be made to enter upon the soul's real immortality in time; then will man be true—1) To God, Who made and redeemed him; 2) to himself, as capable of and fitted for this high destiny.

IV. *A Future.*—In which this eternal life will be exercised and spent; an eternal future, corresponding with eternal life itself: full, glorious, and perfect, as being—1) A sensible manifestation of the Presence of

God. Then shall the King be seen in His beauty. 2) A union with the love of God; dwelling in God, Who is love. 3) A participation in the power of God; through which all things, deeds, and states of being will become possible.

Epilogue.—" This is life eternal" which truly— 1) Completes our being. 2) Subdues death and all man's other enemies. 3) Glorifies God by the fulfilment of His end and purpose in the creation of a nature made after His own image and likeness.

SERMON XXIX.

THE SPIRITUAL IMAGE.

"Whose is this image?"—*S. Matt.* xxii. 20.

Origen.—"All men verily bear an image either of the heavenly or of the earthly; but there is a great diversity in these images themselves, and so looking for each one in yourself, you will find a diversity of image, whether of the earthly in sinners, or of the heavenly in saints. Everything indeed which is done by us in each hour or moment, forms a certain image, and therefore we ought to examine each of our single acts, and to prove ourselves in that work and in that word as to whether a heavenly or an earthly image is painted in our soul."—*Hom.* ii. *in Psal.* xxxviii. *Geneb.* i. p. 300, K, L.

There is an outward corporeal image, patent to all, which it is the business of life to impress upon all men. Feature, dress, gait, manner, speech with its tone, inflection, and accent, all combine to form our outward bodily image. The state of society in which men move; their pursuits in life; their culture and education; are so indelibly stamped upon them, that it is easy for any one of sufficient knowledge and experience to read their belongings at a glance. The life of study begets a countenance which is grave, earnest, and thoughtful; of pleasure, an expression of feebleness and superficiality; of sin, a worn and scared look, which is no untruthful index of the life within. There is also a spiritual image, towards the foundation of which each thought, word, and deed contributes. The experience of life tells no less truly upon the spiritual, than it does upon the bodily nature. If we write our lives upon our faces, we also write that same record in other characters, but just as truly upon our souls. Of a spirit entering the spirit-world, it may well be asked: "Whose is this image?" And if the coin both as to country and to value can be determined at a glance, so likewise can the coin of the soul be read at a glance by other spiritual natures, who on looking at it will be able at once to decipher the image that has been forming upon it during all the years of its sojourning in the flesh. A solemn thought that, "everything which is done by us in each hour or moment forms a certain image." Which image is—

I. *True.*—As the sun is a true artist, and the photograph reproduces every minute character of feature or of landscape which passes through the lens of the camera; as the electric wire delivers at its one end a message precisely the same as that which it received at the other; so does the soul register exactly every emotion to which it has given rise. It bears its own true witness on its own behalf. We may deceive men, we may lull our own conscience to sleep, we may blunt our moral perceptions; we may so confuse the understanding, as to confound light with darkness, bitter with sweet, truth with falsehood; yet the soul is all this time forming itself and shaping itself, so as to present to the All-seeing eye of God, and of the Holy Angels, a true and perfect image of our every thought, word, and deed. This image is —1) True in outline and proportion. There is no chromatic aberration in it; thought, word, and deed, are all recorded in it in their proper and relative proportions. 2) True as to the minutest details. Nothing is omitted, nothing is too trivial to find its record there. 3) True, in the perfect and complete likeness which it gives of the whole temper and current of life.

II. *Enduring.*—The image on the coin, after a certain use wears out, nay, the metal itself may be re-melted and coined anew. This spiritual image is, on the other hand, living and enduring. If the soul be immortal, the form which it takes must be immortal too. It may be glorified by heaven; it may be defiled by hell; but under these altered circumstances it remains the same image still. Extra pains, thought, toil, and care are bestowed upon a lasting work; a building that is to endure but for a few centuries; a book which will perpetuate the fame of the author but for a few generations. How much greater care ought to be bestowed upon a work that will never decay, and will know no end? Hence this eternal spiritual image should be formed with all possible—1) Prayer; 2) thought; 3) earnest endeavour. If so be it may be found worthy of this lasting endurance.

III. *Typical.*—The image on the coin represents a certain king or queen. The spiritual image on the soul is likewise a typical one, representing either Jesus Christ —an "image of the heavenly" King and Lord; or Satan—an "image of the earthly;" yet in both cases retaining the strict individuality of the soul who bears it. In certain lineaments an image of either holiness or sin, yet still a true and living image of that responsible moral nature which gave it birth.

Epilogue.—The master sculptor aims at nothing less than absolute perfection in his figure. Shall the Christian aim at less? His image is not formed of marble, but of his living, loving soul, which he is bound to conform to Jesus Christ.

# SERMON XXX.

ATTEMPTS.

"It had been better for us to serve the Egyptians, than that we should die in the wilderness."—*Exod.* xiv. 12.

Origen.—"These are the words of the soul fainting under temptation. But who is so blessed, who is so freed from the weight of temptation, that no thought of doubt creeps into his mind? These are the words of fragility and temptation. Otherwise it is false—for it is better far to 'die in the wilderness' than to serve the Egyptians. For he who 'dies in the wilderness,' inasmuch as he has been separated from the Egyptians, and departed from the rulers of darkness, and from the power of Satan, has made some advance, although he was not able to reach the whole. For it is better for him seeking the perfect life, to die in the journey, than not to have set out upon the search after perfection."—*In Ex. Hom.* vi. *Geneb.* i. p. 45, B.

An attempt, even if it end in failure, is a certain gain; the effort itself carries some good with it;

whilst the failure of to-day may lead to the triumph of to-morrow. In all things attempts are to be encouraged, since they point out—

I. *An earnest purpose.*—Longings and yearnings towards holiness; towards the good, the true, and the beautiful, are so many God-sent inspirations, and are to be cherished and developed; yet not wholly to be relied on, since many a soul has been lost by resting in the mere desire; by being content to acknowledge present imperfection and sin without making any honest endeavour to amend that unhappy state. An earnest purpose must seek some means towards its realization; it cannot rest satisfied with the acknowledgment of a longing after the better; the idea must pass onwards to its practical embodiment. The earnest purpose of reaching towards the goal as yet unattained implies—1) Careful thought; a planning of ways and means (S. Luke xiv. 25); a weighing of capacity and strength; a due consideration of the difficulties implied in our undertaking. 2) A determined will; that will be turned aside and away from its purpose for no slight cause or impediment. 3) A confidence; founded upon a sense of Divine help being given to bless, carry on, and make the purpose fruitful.

II. *A firm endeavour.*—Better to leave Egypt at any risk, to undergo any amount of privation, rather than remain there; to change the state of life under any circumstances, when that state is subject to the slavery of sin. The present estate of the soul is unholy, unsatisfactory, and incomplete: if possible it must be amended. This endeavour to amend must be firm, so as not to be—1) Frightened by seeming opposition. It must be dauntless in its courage. It must look all possible danger clearly in the face; meet all coming struggles nobly with an unflinching eye; and still it must press onwards. It will not for a moment expect to walk over a clear and untroubled course. 2) Discouraged by frequent failures and disappointments. It regards each successive obstacle that has been overcome as another victory which has been gained; as one more step in advance. The Christian life is one long series of conflicts and victories. 3) Weakened or wearied out by the length of the journey. It husbands its strength; it holds on bravely, having prayed for and received the gift of perseverance. By some such course as this, each soul has travelled which has gained the confines of the higher life.

III. *A mighty gain.*—True, the Promised Land is after all not reached; the goal is still not attained. Is all the good purpose and endeavour lost in consequence? Surely not. 1) It is much to have renounced the old life; to have freed ourselves from old enemies; to have gained a brighter and a purer air. 2) It is more; to have by this exercise enlightened, disciplined, and purified the soul. 3) It is most of all to have gained the approval of God, and to hear the conscience saying, " He hath done what He could." Out of many things we are bound to seek to gain some, when we should be well pleased were it possible for us to gain all.

Epilogue.—Ever seek to rise to the higher life, and use every effort to escape from the bondage of sin. He quenches Egypt [the world of indwelling sin] who does not do the works of darkness; who drives wicked and impure thoughts from his soul; " taking the shield of faith, wherewith ye shall be able to quench all the fiery darts of the wicked." (Eph. vi. 16.) By this means we can see the Egyptians dead on the sea shore, and Pharaoh drowned, if we hope in and have faith that God will bruise Satan under our feet shortly.

SERMON XXXI.

THE HALLOWING PRESENCE.

" The place whereon thou standest is holy."—*Josh.* v. 15.

Origen.—" 'As Captain of the host of the Lord am I now come.' (Josh. v. 14.) And Joshua, when he heard this, adored and said, 'What saith my Lord unto His servant?' Joshua knew that He was not only of God, but that he was God; for he would not have adored Him unless he had known Him to be God. For who else is 'Captain of the host of the Lord,' unless our Lord Jesus Christ? Joshua is in Jericho; the enemy still held the city, they were not yet overcome; and yet he calls the standing-place 'holy.' How can Jericho be a holy land which is held by enemies? Perhaps this is what is indicated, that wheresoever 'the Captain of the host of the Lord' may come, he sanctifies the place. Jericho itself was not yet a holy place; but when 'the Captain of the host of the Lord' comes there, it is spoken of as a holy place. I also dare something further, and say that the place in which Moses was standing (Exod. iii. 5) was not in itself a holy place, but, because the Lord was standing with Moses, the Presence of the Lord had sanctified the place."—*In Jesu. Nave. Hom.* vi. *Geneb.* vol. i. p. 183, D. E.

Wheresoever Jesus is, the place becomes hallowed; His Spiritual Presence surely brings a consecration with it. It is this blessed Presence which hallows the Eucharistic bread and wine, the water in the font, the house of God, the several forms of prayer, the ordaining hands of the Bishops with the presbyters. As the sun cannot shine in any spot without illumining and making beautiful the landscape, so does the Presence of Jesus beautify, glorify, and hallow the commonest places, things, actions, and persons of this our common daily world and life. The heart, by its weakness, indifference, sin, and rebellion, may have been an unhallowed and common place enough; but when Jesus has come into it by His Sacraments, Word, or Spirit, it becomes changed altogether; for "the Presence of the Lord had sanctified the place." When Jesus comes into the soul He brings with Him an influence of—

I. *Power.*—When He was on earth, the Lord carried His Divine power about with Him wheresoever He went. He never lost it; it accompanied Him always. The unclean spirits felt it at once. (S. Matt. viii. 29; S. Luke viii. 28.) At every place He was able to heal the sick, to forgive sins, or to show some other sign of His supernatural gifts. Jesus was ever working whilst He was on earth. He is still ever working when He enters into the soul. The spirit of Jesus within a man—1) Excites and quickens: all was dead and lifeless there before He came; now all is changed. The old life is despised, a new life is desired; the true bearings and ends of things are seen in a way clearly, as they were never seen before. All the faculties of the mind are aroused; they want to be up and doing; purging out "the old leaven;" putting off the old man; awaking out of the sleep of sin; taking to themselves the whole armour of God. The Master and King of spirits has condescended to man's spirit, and all its faculties are constrained to fall down in adoration before Him. 2) Restrains and keeps the old thoughts and associations of sin under and in due subjection; they are brought into contact with a Presence more powerful, absorbing, and glorious than their own. In time past the heart verily was unholy, but, "the Presence of the Lord hath sanctified the place."

II. *Association.*—Sin is propagated by association. Contact with sin begets sin, just as contact with contagious disease begets disease. Hence the Apostle's quotation from the wise saying of Menander. (1 Cor. xv. 33.) Holiness too is engendered by holiness. Hence the effect which certain holy places, scenes, assemblies, and words have upon the unholy and the depraved. When Jesus enters the soul, He brings with Him all His associations of purity, holiness, goodness, and truth. In the presence of saintliness, the unseemly thought, word, and deed are alike restrained; they would be felt to be unseemly and utterly out of place. So when Jesus enters the soul the "army of the alien" sins is routed and broken up, and the thoughts of evil are forced down into the lowest and darkest recesses and caverns of the heart. This association is of—1) His past life of holy suffering for our sakes. 2) His present living : watching over and pleading for our sins; His longsuffering: waiting to be gracious unto us. 3) His future reign, triumph, and glory: in which we also look forward to having our share. The heart was full of sad and dark remembrances; but Jesus came into it, bringing His holy associations with Him; and "the Presence of the Lord had sanctified the place."

III. *Relationship.*—Man was ever God's creature; made by God, and for God; belonging to God. The Christian man has been redeemed by and made one body with the Lord. This sense of relationship which has been lost by sin, is renewed and invigorated when

Jesus by His Presence hallows the soul; for then man becomes not one body only, but one spirit with the Lord. (1 Cor. vi. 17.) This renewal of relationship acts upon the whole spiritual nature, making it to feel most keenly how unworthy a thing would it be were it to disgrace so glorious a kindred. Therefore does this relationship—1) Ennoble. It removes all that is ignoble and base from the heart. 2) Guards the portals of the soul from many an unauthorized visitor in the shape of temptation. 3) Stimulates the soul to render itself worthy of such exalted connections. It was dead to these considerations, ere "the Presence of the Lord had sanctified the place."

Epilogue.—The soul hallowed by the Presence of Jesus will feel with Jacob: "Surely the Lord is in this place; and I knew it not. How dreadful is this place!" (Gen. xxviii. 16, 17.)

SERMON XXXII.
THE NOBLE RUIN.

"His disciples came to Him for to show Him the buildings of the Temple."—*S. Matt.* xxiv. i.

Origen.—" Afterwards they say to Jesus, as another Evangelist more expressly states, 'Master, see what manner of stones and what buildings' (S. Mark xiii. 1), that they might incline Him to pity towards that place, so that He might not perform that which He had threatened. These words may have been corporeally so spoken, yet morally on this wise. Since the admirable building of human nature is made, that is to say, the temple of God and of His Word, the disciples and other holy men not only then but also now confessing the wonderful works of God in relation to the human formation, intercede before the face of Christ, and beseech Him that He would not forsake the human race on account of their sins, but that His wonderful works should rather move Him to indulgence, than the iniquity of them to anger."—*In. Matt. Tract* xxvii. *Geneb.* vol. ii. p. 83, E.

Our human nature since its fall through sin, resembles a noble ruin, which everywhere exhibits traces of its former beauty and magnificence; and which, even as a ruin, is not wholly devoid of a certain majesty and glory. The remains which still are standing suggest to the mind's eye that which the perfect whole was once. The mind supplies the missing portions of the fabric, and the stately fragments indicate very plainly what the former majesty must have been. So is it with the "noble ruin" of our human nature. From what is left we can judge of that which has been taken away; from its present we can conjecture fairly as to its past. The ruined church, castle, or hall, is destined to undergo a still further process of decay, until at last "one stone shall not be left upon another;" but it is far otherwise with the "noble ruin" of our human nature; since it is capable of a complete and perfect restoration; the means of which are now supplied ready to hand. By His Divine grace, by His example, and by His propitiation, our Blessed Lord will one day present our common nature to the Almighty Father as pure, as glorious, and as godlike as when at first it came fresh from the Creator's hand. Even now, by sacrament, pardon, and instruction, has the process of restoration begun under the heavenly influences and delegated powers of its Divine Architect. Most praiseworthy, therefore, was it for the disciples to call the Lord's attention to it—"See what manner of stones"—that He might be induced to pity and restore, rather than to demolish them and to altogether throw them down. The followers of Jesus Christ had passed beyond the Temple and the sphere of Temple influences, and yet they pleaded for it; influenced by its past magnificence and its former hallowed associations. So does every thoughtful Christian plead for his common nature, and direct the mind of Jesus to the "noble ruin" which sin has left, and intercede with Him for its restoration and acceptance. These "buildings of the temple" of human nature, this ruin of humanity is noble verily in—

I. *Thought.*—The power of human thought is—1) Penetrative. Whither cannot the thought of man roam? By faith it can penetrate into the heaven of heavens, and enter into the sanctuary of the glory and majesty of God. It can picture the unseen; it can reproduce the past; it can portray the future. 2) Productive. One thought generating another, analyzing another, until at last a whole body of knowledge is stored up in the mind. 3) Godlike. As the mind thinks so does man act; for thought is the parent of word and deed; it is the ruler, counsellor, and governor, of the entire man. Reflection makes man akin to God, with Whom to think, to will, and to do are alike one.

II. *Word.*—Words are noble, as being—1) The

exponents of thought, representing its—*a*) expression; *b*) communication; and *c*) definition. They are not symbols only, but they fix and define its meaning; they reduce it to a consistent shape and intelligence. Human nature is but a ruin; but how noble are these ruins: the mighty words of poets, historians, philosophers, the great and holy and noble sayings which have been either uttered or written from the beginning of the world until now! 2) Things. "Words are things," things worthy of all love and reverence, from which an odour of goodness and grace ever proceeds. Many are the words prostituted, and both badly spoken or evilly written; but good and great words are indices as to what language would have been, had tongues never been divided; had man never fallen.

III. *Deed.*—"What manner of stones"? What noble deeds have been done by mankind. 1) Material: of a nature beyond belief, so mighty and magnificent; from the pyramid of yesterday to the railway-station of to-day. 2) Moral: invoking an energy, courage, and sacrifice itself, which truly certifies man to be of the Divine kindred. 3) Showing a power and a progress which it is the prerogative of man alone to possess.

Epilogue.—The more noble the ruin, the greater is the gain by its restoration: hence the work of Jesus Christ can only be appreciated by those who value truly our human nature; not unduly exalting or unduly depressing it, but setting it down as made by God for God, to be glorified for ever with God, by those who rejoice and give exceeding thanks to Him Who at so great a cost has effected so great a restoration of so "noble a ruin" as the nature of the human race.

SERMON XXXIII.
SPIRITUAL VISION.

" In hell he lift up his eyes, being in torments, and seeth Abraham afar off, and Lazarus in his bosom."—*S. Luke* xvi. 23.

Origen.

Marcus [a Marcionite].—" Was ever any one able to see from earth to heaven? It is impossible. Who having lifted up their eyes from earth, nay, rather from hell, is able to see into heaven, even if there was no 'great gulf' between them?"

Adamantius [orthodox].—The bodily eyes are only able to see the nearest objects, but the spiritual eyes range afar. And it is certain that they, having cast off the body, henceforth behold one another with the eyes of the soul. Mark how the Gospel reads: That 'he lift up his eyes.' The word 'lift up' implies to heaven and not to earth."—*Contra Marc.* sec. ii. *Wests.* p. 56.

In various ways education gives a new sense of sight to the body. The botanist, as he walks abroad, notes plants which an experienced eye is alone able to detect; he sees that at a glance which others can discern only when it is pointed out to them. The artist, in like manner, notices features in a landscape which are wholly invisible to the untrained eye; he recognizes a hundred beauties in form and colour, which an undisciplined vision would never be able to observe. Education is capable of bringing the several senses of the body to a high state of perfection. To the deep and calm thinker abstract truths take a concrete form, and become actual, well-defined verities. To the poet, and to those who cultivate the imagination, events of the past are presented to the mind as clear and as distinct as the actual occurrences of the present; more than this, the cultivated imagination can invent, and conceive, and describe, so that the products of the brain become to themselves and to others substantive realities. If all this be true of earthly things, it is eminently true of things heavenly. God's prophets of old were at the first called "seers" (1 Sam. ix. 9); for they saw, being illumined by the light of God's Spirit, things which were hidden from the common gaze. They were enabled to penetrate that veil which God has seen good to place before the future. Faith in the soul gives a new sight to the mind, and reveals to it, as in a mirror, the deep things of God. Inward holiness brings an inward vision with it. The leading of God the Holy Ghost does in an infinitely greater degree for the soul, that which human education does for the development of the bodily vision. The range and extent of the spiritual vision is indicated in this history of Dives and Lazarus; the disembodied soul of the rich man partaking of a power of spiritual vision which is well worthy of consideration as touching upon what our own faculty, in this respect, may be after death. The attributes of spiritual vision in the body now may be said to indicate that such vision will be—

I. *Boundless.*—There is a limit to the bodily vision even when aided by the most powerful glasses; but the spiritual vision is confined to no limitation of space. In proportion as the eye of faith is illumined by Divine grace, so is the extent and range of its vision. This vision looks over and beyond the hills of sin and sorrow to that everlasting hill whence comes the soul's true help. It is boundless in—

1) Extent. It embraces life and its dark providences; the past with all its manifold changes and contradictions: the present with its infinitude of hopes and fears. The "eye of faith" sees not one point of the horizon alone, but all around it. The view is taken from a Pisgah height unto which the soul has been lifted by God's grace. 2) Depth. It looks far below the mere surface of things; tracing Divine providences from their first unfoldings to their issues; unmasking the conventional views with which education or a par-

ticular aspect of civilization invests things. 3) Effect. The vision reacts upon the recipient of it; and according to its glory and its wonder, does it move and influence the whole of the inner man. The "eye of faith" in this respect far transcends the eye of reason. The former may accompany the latter for a short portion of its course; but the latter soon exhausts the measure of its power, and the former travels onwards into higher and loftier regions alone.

II. *Clear.*—A blurred and imperfect sight is but one remove from total darkness. The man who saw "men as trees walking" (S. Mark viii. 24), was as yet only partially restored to sight. To rightly judge of the forms and relative distances of objects we require a clear eyesight. A thousand circumstances conspire to render the bodily vision indistinct; atmospheric influences; mist and vapour; the insufficiency of light; the condition of the eye itself; are all so many disturbing causes. When the soul has been cleansed, purified, and illumined from above, it sees with a clearness which is free from any admixture of —1) Weakness. Being strong in the hold which it has upon heavenly and eternal things. It can examine without flinching the glory of the Sun of Righteousness; beholding the face of God's sky. 2) Error. One object is not mistaken for another; light is not mistaken for darkness, nor bitter for sweet. (Isa. v. 20.) Things are seen clearly as they are. 3) Hindrance. No mists of passion or prejudice arise to obstruct the view, and to darken that which God ordains shall be most clear to the faithful soul.

III. *Real.*—The untutored eye, in examining a landscape for the first time, or on its first glance into a microscope, sees in both cases many objects which have no existence there; shadows and semblances are taken for realities. In the intellectual vision, too, motives and delusions which are but apparent are presented to the mind as indisputable truths. Hence the hold that mere opinion has upon so many men. The spiritual vision, the product of faith, deals with the real alone. It beholds the devil as a real person; sin as substantial; heaven and hell as local states and places. It invests with a distinct personality each Christian grace. This vision is real as showing—1) Eternal realities; things which the resurrection body will also acknowledge. 2) A present course of life and action. 3) A future state which will last for ever.

Epilogue.—Darken not by sin this spiritual vision. Close not the eye of the soul to the revealings of God's mind, which enlighten the dark pathway of this life. Bear in mind the Divine saying. (S. Matt. vi. 22. 23.)

SERMON XXXIV.
HOLY DISCIPLINE.

"If thy hand or thy foot offend thee, cut them off, and cast them from thee: it is better for thee to enter into life halt or maimed, rather than having two hands or two feet to be cast into everlasting fire. And if thine eye offend thee, pluck it out and cast it from thee: it is better for thee to enter into life with one eye, rather than having two eyes to be cast into hell fire."—*S. Matt.* xviii. 8, 9.

Origen.—" The hand is understood to be the act of the soul sinning; and the foot, the walk of the soul sinning; and the eye, the sight of the soul sinning; which it behoves to cut off, if they cause offence. For frequently in Scripture the works themselves of the members are expressed by the members, as, 'My hands also will I lift up unto Thy commandments.' (Ps. cxix. 48.) We 'lift up' not the hands themselves, but the work of the hands to the commandments of God when we do works worthy of God. And, 'Unto Thee lift I up mine eyes.' (Ps. cxxiii. 1.) Not these eyes, but the mind which sees through these eyes. Again, 'I turned my feet unto Thy testimonies.' (Ps. cxix. 59.) Not the feet, but the motions of the soul are turned to the testimonies of God when we may have begun or may wish to live according to God. All of which powers, that is, sight, act, and walk, ought to be cut off if they are evil, that so without them we may enter into life; not doing what we desire, rather than that fulfilling our own wills, we may enter into the fire. And in the first place, it is a blessed thing to abstain from all offence; that no power of the soul may be taken in evil, but that we may use all for good. For so with two feet, and with two hands, and with two eyes, of the body and the soul, we may enter into eternal life."—*In Matt. Tract* v. *Geneb.* vol. ii. p. 37, D. E.

No loss, however great it may seem to be, is a real loss, if by its means there is gained eternal life. The salvation of the soul stands before all else; everlasting happiness and glory, before any suffering either of mind or body in time. This is the great truth that our Blessed Lord meant to teach men: that no sacrifice is too great to be submitted to, if heaven can thereby be gained. The surgeon may amputate a hand or a foot to save the life of the body, and his work is received with submission, and even thankfulness; how much rather to save the life of the soul should we not be willing to lose a spiritual hand, or

foot, or eye ? This sacrifice of the part for the whole—
of time for eternity; of the present for the future—
was often insisted upon in the teaching of the Lord
(S. Matt. v. 29 ; S. Mark ix. 43-48; S. Luke xvii.
33); it formed a prominent article in His spiritual
code of laws. The three subjects of Holy Discipline
which are especially brought before us in the Gospel
are—

I. *The Will.*—" The act of the soul sinning."
The will is the cause and ground of all human action ;
it is to the soul just that which the hand is to the
body. If heaven is to be gained, the will is to be
disciplined; and if still stubborn and rebellious, it is
to be " cut off " altogether, so that man's will may no
more rule, and God's will alone be allowed to direct
and order the heart. Our Blessed Lord could alone say
truly and utterly, " Not My will, but Thine be done;"
for in Him alone were the human and Divine wills one
and indivisible. The discipline of the rebellious will,
forms one of the hardest tasks of the spiritual life,
since it implies—1) Self-sacrifice ; which is manifested
in its inner and its severest phase, which implies not
a giving up of that only which is outward, and can
easily be dispensed with, or is of small value, but a
renunciation of that which forms part of the soul's own
nature ; of a cherished affection ; of a fond ambition ;
of a stern resolve which is opposed to the loving com-

mands of Jesus. 2) Self-government; the power of bending the inward nature according to a rule which is received from without. The word of Jesus becomes the law of life, before which the will bows down in lowly submission. 3) Self-knowledge; a clear and perfect understanding as to the tendency and bearing of these hands of the soul, and the work in which they are engaged. Let the right hand be cut off, the firmest resolutions be given up, rather than let be hazarded the salvation both of body and soul.

II. *The Reason.*—Which "is the foot, the walk of the soul." By reason the soul proceeds to acquire knowledge, walking by the inductive step, building up a general system from a careful and increasing noting of particulars. This reason, this marching power, this foot of the soul, sometimes carries it into regions which are—1) Forbidden. God has revealed much to man, but He has hidden more from him. Reason sometimes tries to fathom the depths of God's providence; to solve problems the key of which is in His hand alone; to pry curiously into things which God has purposely left concealed. There is a forbidden realm of reason when it becomes an offence and needs to be "cut off," and its walk stayed. 2) Dangerous. Many a path of reason leads to the pit of doubt; to the precipice of danger; to the quagmire of impurity. If reason becomes an offence, then "cut it off" with the knife of faith, and pass beyond it under a sure guidance.

III. *The Imagination.*—Which is "the eye, the sight of the soul;" by which it sees things far beyond the reach of mortal vision; things which are still in the future. The imagination is far-reaching and prophetic; and it causes offence when it—1) Deceives: running riot, picturing the glories of heaven whilst unmindful of the life of holiness on earth; the infinite mercy of God as opposed to His justice; the harmlessness of sin, and the littleness of its punishment. 2) Hinders: leading the soul to despise this day of small things, because of the brilliant visions which it sets before it. 3) Puffs up: by the "greatness of the revelations" which it presents to the soul; engendering a certain pride in itself, as well as a despising of the incidents and powers of this time and life. This imagination causing "offence" must be "cut off" by an application of the sober standard of revealed truth.

Epilogue.—Three conditions are set before men— 1) With two hands, two feet, and two eyes; with unsubdued reason and imagination to go down into eternal death. 2) With one hand, etc., disciplined in all the spiritual powers to gain eternal life. 3) With the fulness of a sanctified will, reason, and imagination, with two hands, etc., both of body and soul, to enter into eternal life.

SERMON XXXV.

THE GRAND RECEIPT.

"That which cometh out of the mouth, this defileth a man."
—*S. Matt.* xv. 11.

Origen.—"Moreover, let us see that the things which go out and pollute man do not do so because they go out, but they hold the ground of pollution in the heart, when they go out of the heart before they go out of the mouth; they are evil thoughts; of which the species are, 'murders, adulteries, fornications, thefts, false witnesses, blasphemies.' For these are they which defile a man when they go out of the heart; and hence egress is made by the mouth; for had they not gone forth out of the heart, but had been confined in that place close to the heart, and refused an utterance by the mouth, they would have soon been abolished, nor further would the man have been polluted. Evil thoughts are the fount and origin of all sin. For if these do not overcome, there will be neither homicide nor adultery, nor any one of those evils. Wherefore 'keep thy heart with all diligence' Prov. iv. 23)."—*Tract* i. *in Matt*. c. xv. *Geneb*. vol. ii. p. 17, B. C.

A receipt which cures some dire and long-standing disease may justly be considered to be of inestimable value. Our Lord's words are, "Out of the heart proceed evil thoughts." (S. Matt. xv. 19.) And the teaching of a great Father of the Church is, that if these evil thoughts are not allowed to proceed out of the heart they soon wither up and die. As fire becomes extinct without fuel; as the lamp dies out if the oil be consumed; so does sin pine away and die if it has no room for expansion, no fresh soil in which to root itself, no fresh faculties upon which to operate. The "occasion" propagates as well as generates sin. Let the "occasion" be denied, and the sin dies a natural and a speedy death. It has nothing upon which it can live. There is something very noble in this prerogative of man; that, with the aid of Divine grace, he can, by the action of his own free will, conquer and utterly slay indwelling sin; that by the power of his will he can subdue his direst and greatest enemy; the sinful pleadings of a wayward and debased soul. All know and practise self-restraint in regard to the body; few happily allow it to run into either a wilful or a riotous excess. The same self-restraint applied to the soul, stays the growth of evil, and goes far towards " perfecting holiness in the fear of God." The application of this grand receipt must be made—

I. *Unsparingly.*—When evil thoughts arise, the will must put them down with an unsparing hand. No exception must be allowed. Many a well-loved but unholy thought will plead for some small indulgence. An old affection will claim exemption from the general edict. A particular cast of thought, leading to discontent, indolence, or harsh judgment of others, will assert that it has become part of our nature, and besides is not after all so very sinful. But in no single case is the stern discipline to be relaxed. The harder the task of repression the greater is the victory which is gained over conquered sin; the more complete is the remedy. This sternness of application demands that the action of the mind be under all circumstances —1) Impartial : dealing alike with every kind of unholy or of un-Christlike thoughts. 2) Courageous : not shrinking from a little suffering and even from severe discipline; not expecting to gain so great a result without corresponding pains and labours. 3) Thorough : not caring to deal with half measures, but willing to part with a right arm or a right eye, so that the great and glorious end be attained. Sin can thus be practically subdued by a stern repression and by the exercise of an unflinching discipline.

II. *Continuously.*—Evil thoughts are ever ready to arise, and when checked only bide their time to spring up again into a new life and vigour. Let the policy of repression be relaxed even for a day, nay, for an hour or for a moment, and sin in one of the many forms of thought is the result. The heart as well as the mouth must be guarded without any intermission. This continuous self-restraint demands—1) Watchfulness : it must be untiring in its energy and cautious in its operation, so as to be never deceived or beguiled. 2) Self-knowledge : so as to know and to feel by the instincts of the conscience and the impulses of the soul when the thoughts are going astray. 3) A standard : to become a rule of life and of faith ; the deviations and conformations to which admit of a plain and decided expression.

III. *Hopefully.*—As being sure of a victory sooner or later. Hope is the mainspring of all success, spiritual, moral, intellectual, and material. The remedy must be applied in the firm hope that it will do its proper work upon the disease. Depressed, anxious, and humiliated we all must be when, thinking upon the sad amount of indwelling sin, we apply the "grand receipt" in the hope that it will by these means be destroyed. This hope includes—1) Earnest desire : a longing and a thirsting for a holiness not yet attained. 2) Earnest endeavour : that which we hope for we strive with all our powers to obtain. 3 Earnest prayer: that our hopes may be crowned with success; being helped by a spirit which is as much holier as it is mightier than our own.

Epilogue.—Why continue in sin? Why be untrue to your new nature; to the purpose of Jesus concerning you? It is in your own hands, by applying "the grand receipt," to "work out your own salvation," even if "in fear and trembling," for it is "God Who worketh in you." (Phil. ii. 13.)

SERMON XXXVI.
CHRISTIAN CULTURE.

"Every plant, which My heavenly Father hath not planted, shall be rooted up."—*S. Matt.* xv. 13.

Origen.—" Therefore God plants; and there is a certain particular agriculture of God, and it is needful that this field which God cultivates and plants should not have one species of tree [only], but like the country of a rich and powerful husbandman should be well furnished with the germs of every kind of shrub. But how all things ought to be ordered in the field of God, we should consider from the fields of this world which men cultivate. Does the *Paterfamilias* husbandman in his own field have all vines, or all figs, or all apples, or all palms? But does not he who is a diligent and industrious planter have his field planted and well furnished with all these? If therefore we can understand, in the field also which God plants there is not one species alone of trees which only bears sweet apples, but some sweet and others sour."— *Hom. in Lib. Reg. Geneb.* vol. i. p. 221, C.

The human soul is a fruitful soil. It is always producing. The circumstances, needs, and associations of life are ever casting seed into it, which seed is watered by the thousand varied influences which pass over the mind as rapidly as thought itself. As the wicked soul can well be called the garden of Satan, so the Christian soul can be regarded as the garden of the Lord, in which Jesus the heavenly Husbandman is ever so working by His Spirit and by His grace, that the trees—the thoughts, intents, purposes, and desires of the soul—may be of the proper genus and species, and that they may be so tended that they may bring forth their due fruit unto everlasting life. All knowledge that is true and real is a purifier of the heart: inasmuch as it disciplines the understanding it elevates the conscience; it subjects and restrains the lower appetites and passions. Therefore secular and religious knowledge are both handmaidens of the same Master; the former preparing the soul to receive larger measures of Divine grace, and to enter more keenly and deeply into the sublimities and mysteries of the faith. As a rule, the most one-sided, bigotted, and defective views of Divine Truth are taken by those who have limited their studies to specially religious subjects; and thus have deprived themselves by their own narrow-mindedness of the power of mounting to any eminence of height, from which can be descried the greater glory of God. The bitterness of religious sectaries is in a direct ratio to their want of mental culture. In the Garden of Eden in addition to the "Tree of Life," was "the Tree of knowledge of good and evil," and many other varied and beautiful trees besides, all of which added to the glory and completeness of this Paradise of Delight, where—

> "Overhead up grew
> Insuperable height of loftiest shade,
> Cedar and pine and fir and branching palm,
> A sylvan scene; and as the ranks ascend
> Shade above shade a woody theatre
> Of stateliest view . . . . . .
> a circling row
> Of goodliest trees, laden with fairest fruit;
> Blossoms and fruits at once of golden hue."
> —*Paradise Lost*, Book iv. 137-148.

The elements of the culture of the Christian mind ought to be—

I. *Varied.*—There is an infinite variety in God's creative works: in the seasons, and in the aspects of the sun, the clouds, and the sky, changing as they do from hour to hour. More subtle variety still, is to be found in the human mind in its several instincts, aspirations, conceptions, and experiences of things. The body does not thrive upon one kind of food alone; and for its continuance, the mind in the same way requires a varied mental diet, if it is to be preserved in a healthy condition. This very variety of culture gives the mind—1) Freshness. Bringing it for a time into a new sphere of thought, and placing it under new circumstances and relationships. 2) Rest. Change of position is rest to the sick body; change of employment affords comparative rest in manual labour; change of the current of thought rests the mind by engaging and bringing into play, for the time, a new set of faculties. 3) Reparation. We love home, yet still we take a "change of air." We return to it again with stronger feelings of attachment and affection than we had before. So we love spiritual meditation. Our true home is the mind of Jesus; but we turn for an interval to the mind of man, and then fall back again with a renewed love and energy upon the study of the Gospels.

II. *Representative.*—In Jesus Christ are summed up all the treasures of wisdom and knowledge. (Col. ii. 3.) He represents in His own person God, heaven, and human perfection; so ought the Christian mind to be a representative one: representing—1) The Godlike thoughts of many minds past as well as present. 2) Phases of character which unite the excellences of the many, with the imperfections of the few. 3) That wisdom of the Spirit which accompanies His sevenfold gifts.

III. *Subordinate.*—Although varied and representative, the elements of Christian culture ought to be subordinate to the culture of the spiritual life, which is the produce of—1) Faith working by love. (Gal. v. 6.) 2) Holiness in thought, word, and deed. 3) A soul waiting upon God (Ps. lxii. 1), to be taught by Him; submitting all things to His will, and using all knowledge to His honour and glory.

Epilogue.—The Christian is the highest style of man, and he should partake to the full of his proper share of the knowledge and accomplishments which make up the culture of this world; and in addition to this, "the Tree of Life" should grow in the field of his soul; whilst from his Pisgah of faith he looks onwards and forwards to the heavenly Canaan. Not despising earthly culture, he subordinates it to the heavenly teaching; and bides in faith and patience until the time when he shall be wholly and for ever "taught of God." (S. John vi. 45.)

SERMON XXXVII.
THE MORAL PRESENCE.

"I live: yet not I, but Christ liveth in me."—*Gal.* ii. 20.

Origen.—" This was the language of one disowning himself, of one putting aside his own life, but of one who has received Christ into himself that he might live in Him as righteousness, and as wisdom, and as sanctification, and as ' our peace,' and as the power of God, working all things in Him."—*Commen. in Matt. Huet.* vol. i. p. 288, B.

How does Jesus Christ live in the souls of the faithful and become their true life ? This is a deep and solemn question, one moreover which has received divers answers. The whole body of the Catholic Church says, by maintaining a sacramental presence in the soul ; that the worthy recipient of the Sacrament of the Altar receives Jesus Christ Himself, spiritually, really, and substantially ; first into his body, afterwards into his soul. Others—the various sects and their heresiarchs—affirm, that by a dreamy, hazy, imaginative faith, by a kind of undefined belief in Him, He becomes present in a spiritual and mysterious sense to the heart; or rather He is represented there. Lastly, many regard Jesus Christ as the perfection and personification of all the Christian graces. They declare that Jesus Christ is not merely righteous, but that He is Righteousness; not merely wise, but Wisdom; that He is not the possessor of an abstract grace, but the Personification of such grace in a concrete form. Jesus Christ, assert they, is humility; and when I become humble the humility of Jesus dwells within me: when I am true the truth of Jesus dwells within me. So that with every successive spiritual adornment the soul receives a new "Moral Presence" of Him in Whom dwelleth all the fulness of the Godhead bodily. (Col. ii. 9.) Because man is imperfect here on earth, he now can enjoy only a partial Presence of His Lord; but when he shall have become holy as He is holy, he will enjoy this blessed Presence in its fulness and perfection. These three explanations of the Presence of the Lord in the heart can be distinguished as sacramental, virtual, and moral. This "Moral Presence" which may be either united with or caused by the Sacramental Presence, may be stated to be—

I. *Plain.*—It cannot be misunderstood. There cannot by any possibility be any mistake as to whether Jesus is or is not present in the soul. If the "mind of Christ" is in a man, the Presence of Jesus Christ is in him too. When an absent loved one is perpetually being imitated, in thought, word, and deed, there can be little doubt about the fact that the memory of that absent one is fresh, green, and active within the heart. So if there are certain things which are contrary to flesh and blood which Jesus Christ alone can teach, the manifestation of any or of all of those things is a proof which is nearly sure as to—1) Who the Teacher is. 2) The place in which He is. 3) The work which He is now doing there. "I live;" I am becoming like Jesus Christ; yet after all, it is "not I, but Christ liveth in me."

II. *Practical.*—This "Moral Presence" goes beyond a dreamy confession of faith, which has either no or at best a very small influence upon the life. Our Blessed Lord said of the false prophets, "Ye shall know them by their fruits." (S. Matt. vii. 16.) So are men ever known by the fruits of their lives, which are expressed in word and deed. Indwelling righteousness makes a man righteous in thought, word, and deed; indwelling wisdom makes him wise; indwelling sanctification makes him holy; and so of all the other Christian graces. Jesus Christ living within and quickening the inner man with His blessed Presence produces a Christ-like life; reproduces on a feeble and imperfect scale His own human life on earth, which He led whilst tabernacled with us in the flesh. When the Presence of Jesus Christ comes into the soul He produces a new life of—1) Thought; 2) Word; 3) Action. "Behold," saith He, "I make all things new." (Rev. xxi. 5.) Old sins are banished; old errors are cast away; old doubts are dissipated; all men can take knowledge of such that they have been with Jesus. (Acts iv. 13.) "I live" in holiness, self-sacrifice, love, humility, and faith; "yet not I, but Christ liveth in me."

III. *Progressive.*—It comes into the soul as the sun arises upon the earth at morn. There is a faint streak of light upon the horizon, then a twilight; afterwards by little and little, by slow degrees, does the sun come into view and gild all creation with the glory of his newly-risen light. So by degrees, progressively, does Jesus Christ come into the soul. He comes in the form of one grace; then in the form of another; until he has fully come; when there is not another grace to be gained, and so in His perfection He comes not during this present life. Still there is a progressive presence in the souls of all those whose path shineth more and more until the perfect day. This progressive presence accords with the progressive nature —1) Of the Christian life; which is a going on to perfection. 2) Of the schemes of nature and of providence; which are one continual unfolding of the wisdom and of the power of God. 3) Of the human soul; which inclines ever to forget the things that are behind and to reach forward unto those which are before. "I live," progressing from day to day, growing in grace, nearing heaven; "yet not I, but Christ liveth in me."

Epilogue.— Learn—1) The inestimable value of this Blessed Presence. 2) That it is ever given to those who desire it and seek for it. 3) The infinite loss both for this world and the next which they experience who live without Jesus.

SERMON XXXVIII.

THE HOUSE OF JESUS.

"Jesus sent the multitude away and went into the house : and His disciples came unto Him."—*S. Matt.* xiii. 36.

Origen.—" When Jesus was with the multitude He was not in His house. The multitude was without the house, and it was of His love and benevolence towards men that He left the house, and went out to those who could not come to Him. Afterwards, when He had sufficiently discoursed to the multitude in parables, He sent them away, and 'went into the house,' where His disciples, who had not remained with those whom He had dismissed, came unto Him. Whosoever indeed with a purer mind hear Jesus, first follow Him, afterwards ask where He has His house, are invited that they may see Him; coming, they see and remain with Him ; all indeed that day, but some of them it may be longer. Therefore we also if we desire to hear Jesus, not after the manner of the multitude, but after the manner of those whom He allows to enter the house, receiving something particular beyond the multitude, may be established as servants and domestics of Jesus; that like His disciples we may approach Him after He has come home; and drawing near may ask to be taught; but that it may be more fully understood, that which the house of Jesus may intrust to us, let some one gather up from the Gospels whatsoever things are spoken of the house of Jesus, whatsoever He may have said or done therein; for these heaped together into one mass, will convince such an attentive reader that the things which are written in the Gospels are not only simply [*simpliciter*] written as some imagine, but on account of the simple [*simplicibus*] according to the economy, are put forth as simple [*simplicia*]. But they who desire more acutely and are able to strain their ears, for those, there are hidden there things of great wisdom and worthy of the Word of God."—*In Matt.* c. xiii. *Geneb.* vol. ii. p. 3, B. C.

Holy Scripture may rightly be termed the "House of Jesus;" His Presence is in it; the impress of His mind can be traced directly or indirectly by type and prophecy upon its every page; it reveals His mind and will; it presents us with a living portraiture of Himself; it contains the record of that which He did and said during His three-and-thirty years' sojourn amongst us in the flesh; it is the house or home of His earthly sayings and memories: enshrined there as in a "Holy of Holies," is the loving, living, suffering, pleading, yearning heart of Jesus. Do you want to know Him? you will meet Him there. Do you want to understand the full purport of His gracious words and works? you will learn it there. It is His house consecrated by His Spirit, just as heaven is now His dwelling-place, the place of His sojourning in His ascended Body. It is not until we live with a person for some time that we can be said to know them; to understand their particular looks, ways, words of speech; become, in short, so familiarised with them, that what may appear in them strange to others, becomes quite natural to ourselves. Holy Scripture is then the " House of Jesus," and if you would be beyond " the multitude," you must enter into this house and there abide; not merely for a day or for an hour, but for all your lives long. In other words, Holy Scripture must be studied—

I. *Continuously.*—It is only by abiding continuously in a house that you can learn the character of its inmates; passing, flying visits would never reveal this. Much more true is it of the study of any book or author. At first the study is strange; there is no bond of sympathy between the author and the student; by slow degrees the style and phraseology become familiar, and having become familiar are naturalized in the mind. Longer time is required ere the spirit of the writer and the reader are blended into one. Yet until this process has been accomplished, and a common bond of sympathy has been drawn between them, no one can be fairly said to have entered into the house of his author. Holy Scripture is an inspired house; not built by mere human hands; containing no mere human presence; furnished with no earthly furniture; and a continuous residence is therefore all the more necessary if the mind is really to inhabit this "House of Jesus." It is only by perpetual, prayerful study that "the mind of it" can be translated into the mind of man; that the leaven of Scripture can leaven the inner man; that the soul can be brought from an outward gaze upon the mysteries of the faith to feel and to realize their esoteric force and meaning. Such continuous study must be made—1) Daily. Else the soul loses the tone and temper which the Sacred Oracles had impressed upon it. 2) Throughout life. So that the spirit of Revelation may be intertwined and intermingled with all the varying pulses and emotions of the mind. 3) Naturally. Not in any constrained or forced condition of feeling, but just as we pass from room to room in the house in which we take up our abode. By this continuous study, and by it alone, can the mind become familiarized with the house and its Master, and become as one admitted within, and not like the multitude be kept at the door without.

II. *Diligently.*—In the "House of Jesus" none can afford to be idle; there is so much to be learnt, there is nothing that is unimportant; nothing that is unworthy of observation. The smallest hint that is dropped; the simplest possible allusion; the apparently most common-place circumstance; will, when duly pondered upon and compared, be found to contain the germ of some valuable truth beneath the surface. It is only by such minute and accurate observation that the soul can be made thoroughly at home in the "House of Jesus;" can be made to feel the full significance and value of its gaining an entrance there. Our Blessed Lord never spoke a word in vain; never performed even the slightest action without a purpose. That which it behoved Him either to say or to do, it surely must be profitable for His followers to note and reflect upon. This minute and accurate study of Holy Scripture demands—1) Great care and attention. The sacred page must be read in no hasty or irreverent spirit. 2) Frequent repetition. "Line upon line, precept upon precept, line upon line;" over and over again; ever pressing the grapes for a further vintage. 3) Careful comparison. Noting and comparing the several versions of "the one Gospel;" the different lights in which the same saying or fact is viewed. Hence the urgent need there is that small portions only of the Bible be studied at a time.

III. *Lovingly.*—His disciples came unto Jesus in the house because they loved Him; because they longed for His Presence; because they felt alone and astray without Him. Love is the key to the entrance of that house; no unloving soul can enter therein as a guest. Our houses are entered by those who are not our friends from motives of gain, curiosity, or other business; but such persons are not dwellers in them. Jesus must be loved in order to be known; and the more He is known the more will He be loved. Coming as a faithful, loving disciple into this "House of Jesus," there will be left in the soul no spirit for idle—1) Curiosity. A mere desire to explore the wonders of the place. 2) Cavil or doubt. Taking exception at anything which may be met with there. 3) Contempt. For the humbleness of some of its furniture.

Epilogue.—Considering that the "House of Jesus" contains precious, priceless treasures—all the treasures indeed of wisdom and knowledge—who will be content to stay with the multitude without, and not seek to enter into this "House of the Lord"?

SERMON XXXIX.
THE CONSENT TO SIN.

"Neither give place to the devil."—*Eph.* iv. 27.

Origen.—"'The children of Israel did evil again in the sight of the Lord, and the Lord strengthened Eglon king of Moab against Israel.' (Judges iii. 12.) You see that sins furnish strength to the enemy, and that when we do evil in the sight of the Lord and forsake Him, then our enemies are strengthened by the Lord; then strength is given to the contrary powers. Or if you seek this according to the letter, you will so find that our sins could not become more powerful unless we endowed them with strength; or if you should consider it in spiritual things, the contrary virtues likewise would not grow stronger against us, nor could Satan himself prevail anything against us, except we furnish him with strength through our sins; he would be exceedingly weak against us unless we made him strong by sinning; unless through our sins he could find a place of entering in and ruling over us."—*In Jud. Hom.* vii. *Geneb.* vol. i. p. 213, D.

Each act of the will giving a consent to sin is an admission of the principle of sin into the heart; it implies the giving of a certain place in the soul to the devil, who is the author of sin. Sins committed against the will may be deadly; they may entail much punishment; and they may have been committed whilst yet the cry of "No surrender" has been sounding in the soul; yet their indirect action upon the spiritual nature is not nearly so sad as that which is exercised upon the soul by the smallest transgression which is committed through the agency of the will. Hence the sin of Adam was incomparably greater than that of Eve; for "Adam was not deceived" (1 Tim. ii. 14), whilst Eve was deceived, and fell through weakness. With regard to the consent to sin, even in the smallest matters, we note that it—

I. *Weakens.*—Every bad habit becomes a cause of weakness to the body, and every sin produces a corresponding weakness in the spiritual nature. Humanly speaking, our Blessed Lord was so strong because He was absolutely holy; He was invincible against sin because sin had never gained an entrance into His soul. He well knew what sin was; he was sorely tempted by it; but He never gave way to it, and therefore His power over it was complete. Keep the water entirely out of the vessel and all is right; one little leak soon multiplies itself, and the whole hulk of the ship becomes in time rotten and worthless. As long as the soul is sin-tight, so long is it strong. Hence it is that after having once fallen into sin the second fall is so much more easy than the first; that from successive falls the habit of sin is gained and fixes itself upon the heart with an iron grip. The consent to sin weakens—1) By familiarizing the mind with sin. Causing it to accept as a matter of course that which before such consent would have filled it with loathing and horror. 2) By multiplying the occasions of sin. With such consent being granted, it does not need any great or signal temptation to cause a fall. 3) By increasing the desires of sin. Once let evil thoughts prevail they will be both indulged in and longed for; whilst the more they are indulged in the more will they be longed for.

II. *Arms.*—The consent to sin supplies the adversary of the soul with fresh arms or weapons to be used against the sinner, who fabricates those very instruments which work his own destruction. The three great arms of sin which acquire an almost irresistible power over the consenting sinner are—1) Persuasion. At first the delusive accents are disregarded, then they are listened to, and finally they are accepted and acted upon. Having been victorious once, a second and succeeding victory becomes more than a probability. 2) Occasion. The will consenting to sin, Satan finds most readily an occasion or opportunity for its gratification; in his evil purposes fulfilling to the letter the old proverb, "Where there is a will there is a way." 3) *Imitation.* Satan sets before the mind of the willing sinner the examples of other sinners who have sinned far more grievously than himself, with apparent impunity and success. Quoting the example of David's sin, without making any record of David's repentance.

III. *Betrays.*—The consent of the will to sin betrays the sinner in regard to his sin, in the several matters of its—1) Guilt. The consenting will tries and argues the matter with the conscience, making little of that which God has made much of; saying in the language of the tempter of old, "Ye shall not surely die." (Gen. iii. 4.) 2) Extent. The consenting will pleads for this one little sin, and for this one only; not for a whole course of disobedience to God's law. Satan knows full well that sin is like a torrent, when once the flood-gates are opened the course of the water cannot be further stayed. 3) Issues. The consenting will promises to the sinner all gain or pleasure, immunity from punishment or harm or loss; whereas in this life, as well as in the future, a most heavy penalty is inflicted for the transgression of any of God's holy laws, spiritual, moral, or physical. "Be sure your sin will find you out;" here as well as hereafter.

Epilogue.—Remember, since the grace of God has

come, to the Baptized Christian, that there is no excuse for sin; and that all sin is now voluntary and willingly committed; since if the unaided will is not strong enough to resist, God has promised to give His grace, which will overcome nature, enabling the victor over sin to say: "I can do all things through Christ Which strengtheneth me."

SERMON XL.

THE CARE OF JESUS.

"A certain Samaritan as he journeyed, came where he was: and when he saw him, he had compassion on him."—*S. Luke* x. 33.

Origen.—" The man therefore who went down from Jerusalem to Jericho (S. Luke x. 30), because he desired to descend, afterwards 'fell among thieves" (id.), of whom the Saviour said, 'All that ever came before Me are thieves and robbers.' (S. John x. 8.) What are the blows, what the wounds, by which the man was wounded? Vices and sins. But it came to pass that by the same way first a priest, afterwards a Levite, 'went down,' who it may be had done certain good deeds to other men, but not to this man who 'went down from Jerusalem to Jericho.' The 'certain priest,' I think to be the law; the "Levite,' I suppose to be the prophetic word. Providence was preserving the 'half dead' by Him Who was stronger than the law and the prophets. This is He who sleeps not: 'He that keepeth Israel shall neither slumber nor sleep.' (Ps. cxxi. 4.) He descends that He may save and guard those about to die; to Whom the Jews said, 'Thou art a Samaritan, and hast a devil. (S. John viii. 48.) Who When He denied that He had a devil, was not willing to deny that He was a Samaritan, for He knew that He was a guardian. When therefore He came to the 'half dead,' and saw him wallowing in his blood, pitying, He came to him, that he might become his neighbour. But that you may know that it was according to the providence of God that this Samaritan descended that he might heal him who fell among thieves, you will learn plainly from the fact, that he had with him bandages and oil and wine; which I think He, the Samaritan, carried with Him on account of this one 'half dead,' and also for others who have been wounded by various causes, and who need bandages, and oil, and wine. He 'set him on His own beast;' that is, on His own body, which is His vouchsafing to become man. This Samaritan 'hath borne our griefs,' etc. (Isa. liii. 4.) He 'brought him to an inn;' that is, to the Church, which receives all and denies her help to none; to whom Jesus calls all saying, 'Come unto Me, all ye that labour,' etc. (S. Matt. xi. 28.) And after He had brought him, He did not leave him immediately, but remained with the ' half dead ' one day in the inn, and healed his wounds ; not alone in the day but also in the night, bestowing His remaining solicitude and industry [upon him]. The ' host ' is the Angel of the Church. The ' two pence ' seem to me to be the conception of the Father and the Son, and the knowledge of the mystery that the Father is in the Son and the Son in the Father ; which as rewards are given to the Angel, that he may care the more diligently for the man committed to him ; and he is promised recompense for anything of his own which he may expend in healing the ' half dead.' "—*In Luc. Hom.* xxxiv. *Geneb.* vol. ii. 156, G. H. I.

In this Parable the Lord expresses His care and provision for souls ; and from it we glean that this care is—

I. *Thoughtful or prudential.*—There was forethought displayed in the Samaritan meeting with the " half dead " on the road, and more still in his being provided with the necessary bandages and dressings and appliances for the wounds. All care, to be of avail, must be thoughtful or prudential. The Samaritan might have sympathised sufficiently without his bandages, oil, and wine ; but he could not have rendered the same substantial service to the poor man in his

The Care of Jesus.

distress. This thoughtful care is a recognition—1) Of the needful union of wisdom with affection and pity. Wisdom is needed in any helpful expression of sympathy. 2) Of the value of means. The Samaritan knew that commiseration alone would not bind up, and cleanse, and heal wounds. 3) Of contingent preparation. The Samaritan might have made many journeys without the bandages being needed, and so at length have left them at home, and when most wanted they would not have been at hand. The means of doing good is often lost for want of thought. The Lord planned out His salvation for man with equal wisdom and love.

II. *Personal.*—The Samaritan did not depute others to go and tend the "half dead," but he ministered to him himself. He gave his own personal service, time, and attention to him. He made it his own personal business to succour this one in distress. Hence we learn the value of personal service, which is rendered in the way which is—1) Quickest and readiest. The "half dead" might have died before others could have been found to come to his relief. Others might have been promptly called, but they would have pleaded the need of attention first to their own concerns; perhaps even others might not have been found who would have been ready to go. 2) But who else would have rendered such hearty, cheerful, able aid as the Samaritan Himself did? He was no hireling; his heart was in his work. The "half dead" was his own concern, thought, and care. 3) Most grateful. The "half dead" must have felt far more gratitude for this personal service than if the Samaritan had sent some one to represent him, even at his own cost. Hence we learn never to depute to others that which we ourselves are able to perform. First-handed service is always the best. The Lord Himself came down on earth to seek and to save the lost. The Lord is now Himself pleading for man on the throne of His mediatorial kingdom.

III. *Unselfish.*—1) The Samaritan thought not of himself, his means, time, and trouble; bandages, beast, money were, with his own care, equally devoted to the "half dead." All that was wanted, he for the time most readily gave up for another's use. 2) He looked for neither thanks nor recompense, for that which he was doing he did out of the generous impulse of his own nature. 3) He regarded not the merits of the case itself, as to whether the "half dead" had come to this state by his own fault or folly, and was, or was not worthy of his help. The claim to his compassion was the state in which he found him. So did Jesus give up all for man; looking for no return; unmindful of man's unworthiness and ingratitude. Let your care for others be shown in that you go out of yourselves, wholly and entirely, in helping and ministering.

IV. *Tender.*—The Samaritan did not leave the inn at once, but stayed that day and that night there, still tending the "half dead;" He would not leave him until the crisis of his fate was passed. The tenderness of his care was seen in—1) Watching over as well as in delivering the "half dead" from his present distress. 2) Waiting to cheer and comfort, after the man had been lodged and his wounds dressed; not rendering him the least possible, but the greatest possible, amount of service. 3) Interesting himself in the issue of the event; not willing to pass onwards until assured somewhat of the recovery. With the Lord there is nothing prefunctional, or hard, or harsh; but He is tender, gentle, loving in all His works and ways. A type as to the spirit in which all our help to others should be rendered.

V. *Most needful.*—The traveller would have died had help not been forthcoming;—1) Promptly; any delay would have been fatal. The "half dead" without assistance must soon have died. 2) Efficiently; with a certain skill and knowledge of the needs of the case. 3) Freely; without stint in the manner of its application. Our Good Samaritan cares for our souls in like manner; by His grace helping the sinner quickly, wisely, and bountifully.

Epilogue.—Every means of grace is a token of the care of Jesus. Are such means used—1) Humbly; 2) believingly; 3) continually; for the quickening renewal and purification of the soul? Is the example of the Good Samaritan imitated in its several aspects in your own dealings with others?

SERMON XLI.
THE GOOD BEHIND.

"Had they known it, they would not have crucified the Lord of Glory."—1 *Cor.* ii. 8.

Origen.—"The Cross of our Lord Jesus Christ was double. Does it seem to you a strange and new word, when I say that the Cross was double? that is, it appears to be double for a twofold reason. Because visibly indeed the Son of God was crucified in the flesh; but invisibly on that Cross the devil, with his principalities and powers, was fastened. Will not this seem true to you, if I produce the Apostle Paul as a witness of these things? Hear, therefore, what he himself pronounces concerning them : 'Which was contrary to us, and took it out of the way, nailing it to His Cross; having spoiled principalities and powers, He made a show of them openly, triumphing over them in the wood of the cross.' (Col. ii. 14, 15.) Although other copies read triumphing 'in Himself,' yet the Greeks have 'in the wood.' There is, therefore, a twofold reason for the Lord's Cross : one which is expressed by the Apostle Peter: 'Christ crucified left us an example.' (1 S. Pet. ii. 21); and this second: that the Cross was the trophy of the devil, on which he was crucified and triumphed over. Therefore, and lastly, the Apostle Paul said: 'God forbid that I should glory, save in the Cross of our Lord Jesus Christ; by Whom the world is crucified unto me, and I unto the world.' (Gal. vi. 14.) You see that in this place also Paul has brought forward a twofold reason of the Cross: for he said that two things contrary to themselves were crucified; himself being holy, and a sinful world; according to that form, without doubt, of Christ and the devil, which we have expressed above."—*In Jesu Nave. Hom.* viii. Geneb. vol. i. p. 186, I. K.

The Crucifixion of the Lord Jesus, the world's highest mystery and crowning act of redeeming love, reads to us the lesson of "a good behind," which ought never to be forgotten when judging of the experiences of life. Of all things it was the most impious to crucify and slay the Son of God, the Lord of life and and glory; most unjust to kill " this Man," Who had " done nothing amiss ;" the highest ingratitude to reward with death One Who ever " went about doing good." Yet was there another work going on whilst the Lord was "nailed to the accursed tree:" another crucifixion which the Jews had neither knowledge nor thought of; else, "had they known it, they would not have crucified the Lord of Glory;" seeing that with Him were likewise crucified, "the devil with his principalities and powers, sin and death." The body of sin was crucified with the Body of Jesus on the Cross; death, too, was slain in the dying of the Lord. In this most wicked of human acts there was a "good behind;" and the dark clouds of Calvary had a silver lining, though invisible then to mortal eye. So in all the sorrows of life: its stern discipline; its wasting sickness; its bereavements; its disappointments; there is a "good behind" which is—

I. *Providential.*—Allowed for and ordained by the good, wise, and loving providence of God. Had it not been for the invisible crucifixion of sin, perhaps God would never have permitted the visible crucifixion of His Beloved Son. In all that we here are called upon to bear and suffer, there is also a providential "good behind," which has been both foreseen and provided for by our Heavenly Father and our God. Affliction is backed by glory (2 Cor. iv. 17); death by life (S. Matt. xvi. 25); chastisement by reward (Heb. xii. 11); humiliation by honour (S. Luke xiv. 10); depravation by recompense. (S. Matt. xix. 28.)

There is a providential "good behind" in the meanest and most unpromising incidents in life.

II. *Indirect.*—Prayer, for instance, has a direct action upon God; an indirect action upon ourselves. Any act of kindness which we may show, benefits another much, but ourselves more in softening the heart, in bringing joy and satisfaction to the conscience. All that we do or say, beyond the immediate object of our action, has an indirect effect by way of example. The direct purpose of the Jews was to crucify Jesus of Nazareth; the indirect purport of their act was to crucify the devil. Seek to connect every dispensation with that indirect "good behind" which takes away its sting, and consecrates it for our acceptance.

III. *Hidden.*—At the time, this "good behind" is unthought of; is never for a moment conceived of as being possible. Past experience of life shows that many bitter trials, which when they occurred seemed to afford just causes for unmitigated grief, had indeed a hidden "good behind" them, which in after events and after years was clearly revealed. This thought should cause us to suspend our judgment upon present events; not to be hasty either to praise or to condemn, but rather to wait for "time, the great revealer," to unfold to us God's good purpose concerning us when He thinks it best. This "good behind" is often hidden, to test—1) Faith in God's promises. 2) Patience in waiting upon God. 3) Endurance; reaping, if the soul faints not, in due time.

IV. *Lasting.*—The "good behind" is often lasting, when the sorrow which went before it is of short duration. It is so with all sacrifices made in time for eternity, with the discipline of the earlier years of life which, as a rule, leads to a prosperous and successful manhood. The knife of the surgeon is bitter in its operation, but it may purchase many subsequent years of a happy and healthful existence. Our dear Lord's visible Crucifixion was soon over; His Body soon taken down from the Cross, and restored to life again; but the invisible crucifixion of the devil and his hosts is going on still, and will go on until the end of all things. Shrink not from temporary sorrow, if it carries with it a " good behind " which contains the elements of eternal joy.

V. *Contingent.*—Not to be separated from the outward visible act. If Jesus Christ had not been "visibly crucified in the flesh," the devil would not have been "invisibly fastened to the Cross." Contingency is the expression of a law of life. In this world there is no good without some contingent evil ; no joy without some contingent sorrow. This life is a middle state; and all the actions performed or suffered therein are capable of a twofold relationship—either with heaven or with hell. Hence we learn that unlimited condemnation belongs not to beings in this present state. The " good behind " is contingent upon present evil.

Epilogue.—May the Cross of Jesus, as carrying a "good behind" it, teach to all the lessons of—1) Submission under trial. 2.) Contentment with the present lot in life. 3) Hope for the future. To be overcome by no trials; never to be swallowed up by the sorrow of the world which worketh death.

SERMON XLII.

THE DESCENT FROM THE MOUNTAIN.

"When He was come down from the mountain, great multitudes followed Him."—*S. Matt.* viii. 1.

Origen.—" The Lord now descending, that is, inclining Himself to the infirmity and impotence of others, pitying their imperfection or weakness, "great multitudes followed Him."—*Hom.* v. *In Diversos. Geneb.* vol. ii. p. 284, H.

This descent from the mountain indicates " Christ, the Pattern Man in sympathy," (Wilberforce "Incarnation," c. iv.) The few, could alone be taught, enlightened, advised, and spiritually healed (Origen) upon the mountain, but it was when He "came down" therefrom that the multitudes followed Him; claimed a share in His words and works; appropriated Him as it were to themselves. The few, possessed Him on the mountain-top; He became the heritage of the many, descending into the plain. And this was so because that descent of His holy Body was typical of another and a deeper descent which was demanded by the economy of His earthly mission; in the fulfilment of which our Blessed Lord descended not from the "Mount of Beatitudes" alone, but from the four mystical mountains of—

I. *Glory.*—The Lord came down from the mountain of His heavenly glory when He " made Himself of no reputation," etc. (Phil. ii. 7. 8.) The change from heaven to earth is one that we, with our feeble knowledge of the Heavenly City, can but dimly conceive of. The contrast is something stupendous between the majesty and the glory of heaven and the humiliation, sorrow, and suffering of this present life on earth. Such a change would crush a nature which was only mortal. It was the Divine nature of our dear Lord that sustained Him under the economy of His Incarnation. It was part of His mission that "great multitudes" should " follow " Him, and therefore it was needful that He should descend from the mountain of glory. The resplendent glory of His Godhead on earth would have been—1) Incongruous, or out of place; as a court dress would be unseemly in the poverty-stricken purlieus of a large city. But small sympathy could exist between a Preacher so glorious and a congregation so poor and humble as the poor unto whom Jesus ministered, and therefore He put aside His glory. 2) Unbearable. The reflection even of His glory in the face of Moses was more than man could bear to look upon. (2 Cor. iii. 7.) At the Transfiguration the vision of His glory was almost more than the disciples were able to endure. Had the Lord showed His glory to men, they would have turned away from Him, as being wholly unable to bear the resplendent majesty of His person. 3) Cruel. As setting off to so great disadvantage the distance between "the Lord of glory" and His fallen creatures; as seeming to be a kind of scorn and mockery of the lowly children of men. Therefore He "came down from the mountain" of glory, that He might be humble with the humble; one to them of their very selves.

II. *Power.*—Those in robust health and strength, who have hardly ever had a single day's illness in their lives, can hardly realize the life and feelings of those who are strangers to health; who are the subjects of weakness and disease, and whose existence is one continued exercise of patient suffering. They have never been subjected to the discipline which ever waits upon bodily infirmity. Therefore, as a rule, the strong are less feeling; less tender; less considerate for others than the weak. Had the Lord not descended from the mountain of His power, He could hardly have had compassion upon the weak; hardly have so fully entered into their failings, trials, and hopes. Therefore, like His servant, "to the weak," He "became as weak" that He "might gain the weak." (1 Cor. ix. 22.) The Lord's descent from the mountain of power showed His purely unselfish soul. It was not for Himself that He became weak; weak in suffering, though not in endurance; weak in the hands of others; weak in resisting the opposition of a harsh and cruel world. He was still strong and powerful —1) Over Nature. He commanded the winds and the seas, and they obeyed Him. (S. Matt. viii. 27.) He healed the sick; restored the blind to sight; raised the dead. 2) Over the spirit-world. Casting out devils; forgiving sin. 3) Both in heaven and hell. Both with God the Father and over Satan, whom He bruised under His holy feet. Powerful indeed was the Lord for all, but Himself; powerful He knew Himself to be (S. Matt. xxvi. 53), yet for the sake of men He became weak. that they might have in Him a High Priest Who could be touched with a feeling for their infirmities. (Heb. iv. 15.) To succour the vast company of the suffering and the weak did the Lord descend from the mountain of power.

III. *Happiness.*—Just as the strong have small compassion for the weak, so the happy and joyous have but little fellow-feeling with the stricken and the sorrowful in soul. In sympathy with our race the Lord resigned the joys of heaven, and He became the "Man of sorrows." (Isa. liii. 3.) Descending from the mountain of happiness the Lord endured the sorrow which is common to our humanity on account of man's

—1) Past loss. Original righteousness; God's favour; immortality; and happiness on earth. 2) Present estate; one of suffering, humiliation, sin, and death. 3) Future prospects; death eternal was before man; and did He not come and give men life? Eternal torment was to be men's portion; and did He not come and give them peace? Hell eternal gaped and opened its mouth for our race; and did He not come and open the door of heaven for men? Therefore did the Lord descend from the mountain of happiness to bless all mankind.

IV. *Immortality.*—There is no death in heaven, nor can death tarry among the heavenly natures. Death is the one shadow cast by sin over the fairness and beauty of life. As heaven is a sinless, so also is it a deathless state. The Lord descended from the mountain of immortality to suffer and to die on earth to conquer death for man, by taking away its—1) Sting; the Lord loving and holy died not only for us but also before us. 2) Power; the Lord rose again and we shall rise through Him. His subjection to a like nature established a community of nature between the Lord and His redeemed.

Epilogue.—He descended from this fourfold mount that with Him and by Him we might ascend. He came down not with us for ever to remain in a low estate, but for us to gain the glory, honour, and immortality that He had with the Father before the world was. Seize Him, cling to Him, in love and obedience, that so with Him you may ascend for ever.

SERMON XLIII.
JESUS THE SUN.
"The Sun of Righteousness."—*Mal.* iv. 2.

Origen.—"As in that firmament which has been called heaven, God ordered two lights to divide between the day and the night (Gen. i. 16), so can it be with us; if we study both to be called and to be made heaven, we shall have lights in ourselves which will enlighten us—Christ and His church. For He Himself is the 'Light of the world' (S. John viii. 12), Who also illumines the Church by His light. If any one so advances that he becomes a son of God, let him 'walk honestly as in the day' (Rom. xiii. 13), as a son of God and a son of light; he becomes illumined by Christ Himself, as the day is by the sun. As the sun and moon illumine our bodies, so by Christ and the Church are our minds illumined."
—*Hom. in Gen.* ii. *Geneb.* vol. i. p. 2. K, L.

"The Spiritual Sun Who is the Sun of Righteousness, in Whose wings is said to be (Mal. iv. 2) healing, illumines and girds with all brightness those whom it has found to be right of heart and standing in the constellation of its splendour; but those who walk obliquely towards it, by necessity also itself does not so much regard obliquely as it despises. For how can they who are perverse receive that which is right?"—*In Cant. Can. Hom.* ii. *Geneb.* vol. i. p. 324, L.

That which the sun is to the natural world is Jesus Christ to the spiritual world; the functions which the one sun performs in the world of nature are exceeded in number and excellence by the other Sun in the world of grace. Of the natural sun we note that—

I. *It is a Centre.*—All the heavenly bodies of our system are placed in relation to the sun; they revolve around it whilst itself remains stationary. The sun regulates their orbits, determines their seasons, assigns their relative periods of darkness and light. Jesus Christ is in like manner the centre of the Gospel System of Divine Grace. His saints can but revolve around Him as their centre; the one grand enduring centre of their hope, love, pardon, and grace. Were the sun to be removed from his place, all would be chaos in the regions of space: when the Sun of Righteousness is deposed from the centre of the soul, all is doubt, confusion, vanity, and ruin. This Sun—

1) Regulates the orbit of the holy. The Holy precepts and example of Jesus determine the limits and

the range of their action; their own law of repentance for themselves, and their law of forgiveness for others; the degree in which they ought to conform to the world; their openness or their reticence with regard to the faith; with a thousand other questions of a like nature, to determine which an answer must be sought to the question, "What would Jesus Himself have said or done under the like circumstances?" Beyond the range of His teaching and example the holy dare not travel. As the sun regulates the motions of the heavenly bodies, so does Jesus regulate the every motion of his saints; they ever hear Him saying, "Without Me ye can do nothing." (S. John xv. 5.) 2) Determines their seasons of growth and decay. Makes the winter of their souls, during which there is but small profit when He goes away from them; and He brings the cheering summer-tide to their souls when he returns nearer to them again. In this life under an entire spiritual winter the soul would die; under an entire spiritual summer the soul would become enervated and weak, and forget that this world was not its rest. 3) Assigns their relative periods of darkness and of light, of day and of night, of prosperity and of adversity, of joy and of sorrow. For as night, bringing its rest with it, braces up both mind and body for the coming day, so does sorrow and temptation brace up the soul to "endure hardness as a good soldier of Jesus Christ" (2 Tim. ii. 3), to "resist the devil" (S. James iv. 7), to wrestle "not only against flesh and blood, but against principalities," etc. (Eph. vi. 12.) May the law of Jesus form the orbit in which every soul of His Mystical Body undeviatingly revolves; neither falling short of nor transgressing its due line or course, but steadily and unceasingly moving around Him as around the soul's true centre; referring to Him its every thought, word, and deed.

II. *It Quickens.*—Without the warmth and light of the sun vegetation could not be quickened, the seed would not germinate, the sap would not rise, the bud —which afterwards expands into leaf, flower, and fruit —would not form. The sun is the quickening power of the natural world; and just so is Jesus Christ the quickening power of the spiritual world. He recalls dead souls to life again; and He renews those who are fainting and ready to die, by His—1) Grace. His Spirit comes down into them, so that whereas they were dead they now live. "Christ liveth in me" (Gal. ii. 20), is that which the once dead one feels when quickened into life. 2) Words. Which are "spirit and life" (S. John vi. 63): for—*a*) they convey a message of life, pardon, and acceptance with God. *b*) A means of life forming the food of souls. Plants and animals take dead matter and convert it into living organisms;

so likewise do sounds and words pass into the living organisms of immortal natures, and become in them a principle of life. c) A means of sacramental life; water, bread, and wine, blessed and consecrated, become the channels of life-giving energy. 3) Works. So full of love, gentleness, and goodness, that they enkindle by their imitation a new and holier life within. All noble and heroic action awakens dormant sympathies, and arouses the best and highest elements of our nature. May this Blessed Sun of Righteousness so quicken our dead souls, that they may awake to new forms of glory and beauty.

III. *It Ripens.*—The sun does more than quicken nature into life; it ripens the fruits of the earth when produced. It would be of no profit if the fruit never reached maturity, and so availed not for the wants of man. God never leaves His work half done: the sun that quickens ripens too. The "Sun of Righteousness" also ripens in the faithful the "fruits of righteousness, which are by grace unto the glory and praise of God." (Phil. i. 11.) A beautiful and lovely sight is it, to watch day by day the fruits of the earth ripening under the genial influence of the warm cherishing sun; but a far more beautiful sight is it to watch the fruits of holiness daily growing unto perfection, fostered by the ripening hand of Him Who loved us and gave Himself for us. (Gal. ii. 20.)

IV. *It never Sets.*—When the natural sun shall have set in the gloom of an eternal night, the "Sun of Righteousness" will shine on—if possible, with increased and increasing glory—for ever and ever. It will never give place to darkness and desolation; Its work of glory will never be done. In the soul of the faithful one It shines more and more unto the perfect day which knows nothing of either night or of morrow. Jesus Christ is the Sun of Heaven as He is the true Sun of earth; the Sun of Eternity as He is the Sun of time. The light from this Spiritual Sun is—1) All glorious; beyond all the shining of this lower sun. 2) Immortal; enduring throughout the countless ages of eternity. 3) All-penetrating; reaching to the utmost confines of the kingdom of the redeemed.

Epilogue.—O, Christian Soul! walk not on in unprofitable darkness; let this Spiritual Sun of Righteousness ever shine upon you, with its centralizing, quickening, ripening, and enduring rays.

SERMON XLIV.

DEATH UNTO LIFE.

"Death worketh in us."—2 *Cor.* iv. 12.

Origen.—" But also 'death' itself which 'worketh in us' seems to me to have three differences. For as in Christ one was the time of death, since it is said, 'When Jesus had cried with a loud voice . . . He gave up the Ghost' (S. Luke xxiii. 46) ; and another, 'When placed in the sepulchre He lay there with the mouth closed' (S. Matt. xxvii. 66) ; and a third, indeed, when sought for in the tomb He is not found (S. John xx. 13), because He had already risen—the beginning of Whose Resurrection was visible to no man ; so also in us who believe this threefold reason of death is to be understood. And first, indeed, the death of Christ is shown in us by confession of the voice, since 'With the heart man believeth unto righteousness ; and with the mouth confession is made unto salvation.' (Rom. x. 10.) Secondly, truly in the mortification of the 'members which are upon earth' (Col. iii. 5), when we are always 'bearing about in the body the dying of the Lord Jesus' (2 Cor. iv. 10); and this is what it says, 'That death worketh in us.' The third, verily, when we rise from the dead, and 'walk in newness of life.' (Rom. vi. 4.) And that we may more briefly and clearly explain: the first day of death is to have renounced the world; the second, to have renounced the sins of the flesh; but the fulness of perfection in the light of wisdom is the third day of the Resurrection."—*In Epist. ad Rom.* c. vi. l. v. *Geneb.* vol. ii. p. 353, D.

The death of the body, as it is the end of earthly ties, work, possessions, desires, and associations, so is it also the beginning of new ties, work, desires, and the rest. Death is a beginning as well as an end; a beginning as really and truly as birth is. The death unto sin, is in like manner the beginning of a new life in the soul. Like bodily death it is at the same time an end and a beginning. Of this spiritual death unto sin, which is but the beginning of a new life, the death of our dear Lord in the body was an earnest and a type. The death of Jesus was not the end but the beginning of His mediatorial work; it was the foundation upon which His mediatorial kingdom was to be raised. In death, as in life, that Lord Whose whole life was one continuous parable of action, became to man a similitude. As there is a death unto death, so there is a death unto life; and the successive stages of this latter death are represented to us by the death of our Blessed Lord. This spiritual death unto life has its three days; of which we note: the first day of death, to the world without; the second day of burial, of our earthly affections and desires, of death to the world within; and the third day, when the soul arises to the new life of grace. Hence this "death unto life," as represented by the death of Jesus Christ, implies a—

I. *Renunciation.*—The world of sin without has to be renounced; " the pride of life " has to be given up. This can only be done when the conviction is forced upon the mind that honours, riches, pleasures, and the like, when they form the sole end of life, are both purposeless and vain. Confession is then made that these things are not really that which they seem to be; that they are transitory; unavailing in the time of the greatest need; and that they fill the soul to the exclusion of that which is best, highest, and alone profitable for its eternal good. The lower must be renounced if the higher is to be gained. In all things it is ordained that a choice and a selection has to be made. This renunciation is—1) Imperative. Our

Blessed Lord said, "Ye cannot serve God and mammon." (S. Matt. vi. 24.) The desires, motives, and actions of the one are essentially opposed to those of the other; no common ground of concord can be found to exist between them. According to the Divine command a choice has to be made. 2) Just. Each master awards according to his kind. "The wages of sin is death" (Rom. vi. 23), "but the gift of God is eternal life." (Id.) We cannot serve the world and God; we cannot accept the wages of sin and of God. It is just, therefore, that a selection be made between them. 3) Congruous. A soldier must belong to a definite army; it is meet that he must wear the livery of some country. All men are soldiers. Jesus or Satan are their respective leaders.

II. *Mortification.*—A death to the world of sin within; to the pleadings of an undisciplined body; to the yearnings and vain imaginings of an unchastened soul. The first day of the confession of sin implies the renunciation of sin in act; the second day of the mortification of the old nature implies the renunciation of sin in desire and in thought. Modification of self is a second step in advance of renunciation of the world; more searching, touching more nearly the "apple of the eye," than the former one. It is signified by our Lord when He rested in the tomb, and therefore it implies a stilling or quieting of the affections. 1) No longer are they to be let to run riot upon earthly objects without either measure or stint. The one object of love with heart, soul, mind, and strength, is God Himself. All other love is to be subordinate to this. 2) Desires; hankering after that which we have not and are not. Many a holy and profitable life is frittered away through indulgence in vain desire; always longing for that which is not; always discontented with that which is. 3) Will; so that in holy submission it may accept God's providential dealings.

III. *New Life.*—Of which our Lord's rising from death was a similitude : the completion of that death unto sin which results in a new and better life. Such new life is an—1) Exchange. Every sacrifice in the cause of that which is good and holy, brings some compensation in its train. In the Gospel, if a man is bidden not to love this world and the things of it, a brighter, purer, and better world is offered to him in exchange. In every way Jesus Christ came to make men richer, not poorer, than they were before. 2) A gain. Spiritually as well as bodily "to die is gain." The new life is so much better than the old; it is lasting, satisfying, ample, and perfect. 3) A triumph and a result. It represents the end and working out of the renunciation and mortification of the world and the flesh; it is a triumph of the spirit over the flesh;

of the immortal over the mortal nature. By dying Jesus conquered death; by dying unto sin, we can also conquer sin.

Epilogue.—Pray that this death unto sin may indeed work in the heart—1) Fully; 2) perseveringly; 3) triumphantly. Then will be fulfilled (Gal. ii. 20).

SERMON XLV.
THE INWARD EYE.

" To one the savour of death unto death; and to the other the savour of life unto life."—2 *Cor.* ii. 16.

Origen.—" But if you are able to understand morally the difference of the Word which is proclaimed both by 'the foolishness of preaching' (1 Cor. i. 21) to those who believe, and in 'wisdom among them that are perfect' (1 Cor. ii. 6), you will perceive that the Word of God has, verily, to them who are newly introduced to the faith, 'the form of a servant' (Col. ii. 7); as they may say, We saw Him, and 'He hath no form nor comeliness.' (Isa. liii. 2.) But amongst the perfect He comes 'in the glory of His Father' (S. Matt. xvi. 27), so that they may say, 'We beheld His glory, the glory as of the Only-begotten of the Father, full of grace and truth.' (S. John. i. 14.) For to the perfect will appear the glory of the Word; that He is 'the Only-begotten of the Father;' that He is 'full,' at the same time, ' of grace and truth;' which he cannot receive who still stands in need of the 'foolishness of preaching.'"—*In Matt. Tract.* ii. c. xvi. *Geneb.* vol. ii. p. 27, E. F.

Our Blessed Lord Himself as revealed in Holy Scripture, and every single truth therein contained, can be viewed in one or more aspects according to the "Inward Eye" with which they are regarded. This "inward eye" is like the sun, which in shining imparts a loveliness and a glow to the commonest landscape, and which in retiring behind the clouds leaves the loveliest prospect dull and incomplete. This "inward eye" is like the tinted glass which, placed before the eye, reduces all colours to a monotonous monochrome. Spiritual and moral truth, persons, places, the circumstances and relationships of life, are all subject to the influence of the "inward eye," and are viewed in strict accordance with its ruling. Hence the mysteries of the Faith become " to one the savour of death unto death;" to another, "the savour of life unto life." (2 Cor. ii. 16.) As bodily taste depends upon the state of bodily health, so does the spiritual, moral, and intellectual vision depend upon the several capacities which influence this faculty. As we are in ourselves, so do we see outward things. Their impressions are really our own. We may note that this reflective vision of " the inward eye " is—

I. *Variable.*—We view life and its several circumstances to-day with different eyes than those with which we beheld them yesterday. According to our present mood and temper so is the appearance of all things to us, whether mental or material. To the jaundiced and the diseased, most things are shorn of their brightness, but they are not ever equally depressing and gloomy. At times we "rejoice in the Lord;' whilst at other seasons, such as those of spiritual dryness, He seems to melt away, and to become hardly more than a mere abstraction to us; and to have lost all power of influencing either the feelings or the life. Bearing this fact in mind, we learn caution, in judging by our feelings of truths which are manifest, and of the first importance. Even the Lord Himself comes before us now as a "Servant," or then as a "King," according to the temporary view of the interior eye. Many great saints have been made miserable, and have doubted of their election, by having mistaken a temporary depression of spirits for a final falling away from grace. In all things, as far as possible, a mean ought to be struck between the depression of the past—day, week, or month—and the exaltation of the present; and a certain correction should be applied so as to bring into harmony those opposing states of feeling; both of which may have their ordained purposes, of reminding man of his mixed nature and relationship; that he belongs to two worlds; and that at present he is placed midway between the two. Here man leads a dying life, and the "savour" both of death and of life are, and must be, his alternating portion.

II. *Contingent.*—Many elements are contained in the one word "happiness;" a thousand contingent circumstances likewise combine to form the vision of "the inward eye." Of these contingent circumstances, some are in our own power; we can either close our eyes to all but the immediate objects of our vision, or we can let them wander hither and thither and so diminish its special effect. Looking directly at a single mountain, the longer it is gazed at the higher and more magnificent does it appear. Take off the eye, survey the whole noble range of hills, and the one single peak loses its first startling effect of grandeur and magnificence. Directing the eye of the soul long and earnestly to the contemplation of some one truth, that one truth grows in dignity and importance; but by letting the mind range over other kindred truths, the firm sharp outlines of the former become blurred and indistinct. The difficulties, apparent inconsistencies, of the human element in the Gospels being considered, the Lord dwindles almost down into "the form of a servant;" the other higher and supernatural side of the Gospels coming before the mind, the majesty and the glory of the Lord appear in all their solemnity and greatness. The Lord meditated upon singly and alone, becomes indeed a great mountain; dishonoured by earthly comparisons and reasonings He sinks down into a little hill, into the " Perfect Man." Learn to make allowance for " disturbing causes" as to the conception of Divine truth whensoever they may arise.

III.—*Personal.*—" The inward eye" colours all things with its own personal tint or hue. There are certain features in the workings and teachings of our Blessed Lord which commend themselves above the others to certain minds; and by such minds our Lord is regarded in the aspect which appeals most forcibly to their own feelings and views of things. In a greater or in a lesser degree our personality is stamped upon our every thought, word, and deed. It influences our judgment, it impairs our rigid sense of justice, and yet becomes a means of strong and holy attraction. To the humble in soul, the humility of Jesus will come home with special power. To the self-sacrificing, this utter forgetfulness of self will bring Him very near to them. To those striving after purity, the glory of His sinless life will have a special charm. The character of Jesus is many-sided, and yet every side has its own peculiar beauty. Jesus has something special for each one; some thought that awakens a deep chord in a particular soul.

IV. *Progressive.*—The vision of the Saviour begins with a sight of Him as He came at His first coming, and will end with the sight of Him as He will appear at His second advent. We need at first " the foolishness of preaching ;" afterwards, "amongst the perfect," we learn to understand the " wisdom of God." " The inward eye," by the discipline of faith, obedience, prayer, and Sacramental communion gains—1) Strength ; 2) Far-sightedness ; 3) Power of discrimination. Strength, to endure the sight of that which at one time it could not behold. Far-sightedness, to extend the range of its vision to the kingdom of God. Power of discrimination, which enables it to discern one spiritual truth from another.

Epilogue. See then that " the inward eye " be kept bright and pure ; that it be constantly and perseveringly exercised ; that it be directed from all that is base and lowly, and that it be lifted up to all that is high, holy, and heavenly ; then will it rejoice at length in ·the Beatific Vision, and will realize Isa. xxxiii. 17.

SERMON XLVI.

THE SHADOW OF LIFE.

"If thou wilt enter into life, keep the commandments."—
S. *Matt.* xix. 17.

Origen.—" Consider, that he who was asking Him concerning the ordained good, was as yet as if beyond the pale of life; so He answers, 'If thou wilt enter into life.' I demand here how any one is beyond the pale of life, and how he may 'enter into life.' By chance in one way, indeed, that man is without the pale life who is without the pale of Him Who said, 'I am the life.' (S. John xiv. 6.) But after another fashion every one who is upon the earth, although he may seem to be most just, is able to be verily in the shadow of life; but not in life itself whilst he is surrounded by the 'body of death,' and is saying, 'Who shall deliver me from the body of this death? (Rom. vii. 24); and is sitting 'in the region and shadow of death' (S. Matt. iv. 16), in that he has not yet come to the land of the living. But any one may enter into life who, abstaining from dead works, is desiring living works; never also speaking dead, but living words, according to the word of the living God; and who has not dead but living thoughts in the heart."—*In Matt. Tract* viii. *Geneb.* vol. ii. p. 46, G.

True life consists in the full development of every faculty, free from any admixture of decay. Can the life of this world develope our every faculty? Can anything, save God, satisfy and develope that mind which bears the reflection and impress of Himself? Imperfection of every kind hinders life. Ignorance, care, toil, sorrow, suffering, disappointment; and sin most of all. A shadow is —1) Unreal. Is man's mere earthly life a real one? Does it deal with the absolutely true, beautiful, and good? Does it lay hold on one thing that is immortal as being imperishable? No; man's "days are as a shadow that declineth." (Ps. cii. 11.) A shadow is—2) Changeable. It is ever altering in size, form, brightness, or dulness. So does the life of man ever change during each portion of his earthly pilgrimage: from childhood to youth; from youth to manhood; from manhood to old age. Changing in expression, thought, feeling, desire, aptitude, and capability. A shadow is—3) Fleeting. It soon passes away and is gone. Man's life is compared by inspired lips to the " morning dew," " a little vapour," and other fleeting and evanescent things. A shadow is—4) Representative. It is the reflection which is thrown by a real object passing between itself and the light; and the form of this object is delineated in the shadow. So is this present life a shadow of that real life which is truly life itself; an adumbration of something far more glorious than itself which is in the background. To the faithful soul in the article of death, "the shadow life" gradually gives place to the real; and whilst the eyes of the body close in darkness, the eyes of the soul awaken to the brightness and glory of a light of life which shall never die. This "shadow life" of man suggests—

I. *The falling of the shadow.*—Before " sin came into the world, and death by sin," man's life was real, and not at all the "shadow life" which it is now. It was real, unchangeable, and abiding; it was the full development of that spirit which God breathed into man's nostrils. The fall took away the substance, and left but its shadow in its place; it cut off communion with the source of life; God Himself, with the objects of life, the knowledge and service of Him; with the reward of life, translation into a higher and more glorious if not into a more perfect state of being. The first falling of the shadow was when the presence of evil came into the Paradise of God; the second, when that presence, like an evil leaven, began to work, suggesting the first thoughts of sin. The third, when the solicitation to sin was listened to, argued about, tampered with, instead of being crushed out of the heart at once. The fourth, when the sin was actually committed, and the true life of the soul—which consists in communion with God—was withdrawn. After this, a formal, physical life remained, which rightly can be called the " shadow of life."

II. *The deepening of the shadow.*—The shadow deepened as men went further and further away from God; as the true ends, aims, and purposes of life gradually passed out of the soul; when not liking to retain God in their knowledge He gave men over to a reprobate mind; when all men's thoughts, words, and deeds, were wicked, their souls were dead in trespasses and sins. As men went down impenitent and blind after a wicked life to an unhallowed grave and gate of death, the " shadow of life " grew in intensity. From the beginning to the end of time, sin ever has, and ever will, take all the joy and brightness out of life; it will throw into shade that which God meant to shine with its own pure light; it will darken knowledge, quench love, uproot faith, eat out and destroy the dignity and beauty of the soul's life. The shadow of one sin resting upon a tender conscience has at times spread its baneful influence over the whole soul, and made " the shadow of life " to become dark indeed. It was a marvellous saying of Infinite Wisdom, "If thine eye be single"—thy heart, the eye of thy soul, be pure—"thy whole body shall be full of light" (S. Matt. vi. 22), and the deepening shadow which sin cast over life shall be exchanged for the real life of the joy of holiness.

III. *The dispelling of the shadow.*—Not for ever was man to be left in the valley of the shadow of death, or to be contented with "the shadow of life;" life itself was to become his portion, when the Life Himself came into this world in order that all men might live through Him, and in Him might have life more abundantly. Jesus Christ changed " the shadow of life," into life itself for man ; slowly but surely He chased away the shades of spiritual death ; restoring to man's soul eternal life, the gift of Jesus Christ our Lord. He came into this world, and by His coming His spirit was given unto men, that they might think the thoughts of life, become filled with holy and heavenly desires, and might see the things which are afar off by the eye of faith. He came, and by His life-giving Presence gave new hopes and promises which were full of life for man. He came, and conquered black death, and opened to man, by His precepts and His pardon, the kingdom of life. The more the mind of Jesus Christ becomes a man's own, the more does the real life of Jesus belong to Him ; He lives for life-giving objects; in themselves a source of life.

Epilogue.—Will you accept "the shadow of life," when the real life is within your reach? Will you rest satisfied with the semblance, when the substance, with all its vast powers and prerogatives, can be made your own?

SERMON XLVII.

THE WORDS OF JESUS CHRIST.

"Never man spake like this Man."—*S. John* vii. **46**.

Origen.—" I think that every word of Christ the Son of God is great, even if it may have been gentle [lenis] ; and the Scripture testifies to this fact; chiefly in those places in which it desires to excite the hearer, that he may pass beyond that which the many can understand and not remain in it; although according to the simple sense I find in it some truth that by some means he can worthily understand on account of the great discourse of the Lord."—*In Matt. Tract* xxxv., *Geneb.* vol. ii. p. 129, B.

Introduction.—One of the greatest of uninspired utterances is contained in the Memorials of Socrates, as recorded by Xenophon. Its teaching is pure, useful, and exalted from first to last. Many of the sayings of the great Philosopher are of infinite value, and immortal in their teaching. The " Memorials " have not inaptly been styled " The Socratic Gospel."

Between, however, this human and the Divine Gospel there is a chasm that cannot be bridged over; there is a difference that no amount of sophistry can either ignore or reason away. "The words of Jesus Christ" stand alone; their echo or like has not ever been heard in the world, either before or since He uttered them. "Never man spake like this Man." The words of the Lord stand alone in their—

I. *Purpose.*—The teaching of the Lord was instructive. He instructed men in all the several duties of life; probing down to their very depths the secret motives and springs of action; setting the glory and beauty of holiness before a sorrowful and a sin-stricken world; awaking new hopes in men's hearts, and filling their souls with a new light. But it was more even than all this: it was a REVELATION; the revealing of an invisible world existing around man on all sides during his sojourn here; of a providence which could be but imperfectly read in the dim workings of its decrees; of a new and of a glorious home, prepared and reserved for immortal natures to abide in when they shall be glorified for ever. "The words of Jesus Christ" were indeed "great" in their purpose, which was to lead man to a knowledge of himself; of God, and of God's gracious intentions towards him both in the present and in the future. This purpose was—1) Eternal; the promises conveyed in the Lord's words are everlasting.

2) Loving; the greatness of the love of Jesus for souls expressed itself in the depth of the regrets which He pronounced over the unheeding and the unloving. (S. Matt. xxiii. 37.) 3) Inflexible; no ingratitude, no coldness, no misrepresentation, could change the tone of the Lord's words. The prayers of the "guest-chamber" (S. John xvii.), and of the Cross (S. Luke xxiii. 34), breathe one and the same spirit. The restoration of a fallen world at such a mighty sacrifice, itself was indeed a great purpose, that invested with a greatness and dignity of its own the words in which it was declared. (S. John x. 18.) Regarding the import and purpose of His words, we must confess " never man spake like this Man."

II. *Simplicity.*—"The words of Jesus" are so very beautiful because they are so very simple. As a great Father observes: "The Lord's sayings were short and concise; He was no rhetorician." (S. Justin.) In their "simple sense" there is always some truth that is patent to all, and which is "profitable both for correction and for instruction in righteousness." It is a sign of greatness of mind to clothe deep and abstruse truths in such plain language that all can gain some knowledge of them. This, beyond all others did the Lord; representing the "deep things of God" in parables, and under similitudes, and by deductions and lessons mainly drawn from the events which were passing around Him. Yet was this simplicity—1) Dignified. There was in it nothing unworthy of a God-sent and Divine teacher; nothing unworthy of the dignity of the message He willed to deliver. 2) Pertinent. The Lord seized upon the salient points of the matter in hand; and these He pressed home to His hearers with due force and illustration. 3) Impressive. No one hearing Him could possibly make light of what He said. Many were convicted; some to repentance and faith, others to rebellion and final condemnation. So "great" are the words of the Lord in their simplicity, that not one of the vast multitudes who crowded round Him need to go away without having gained some good from what they heard. Hence their effect upon the masses. (S. Matt. vii. 28, 29.)

III. *Power.*—(S. Luke iv. 32.)—Uninspired words have often moved men's hearts, and excited in them emotions which were great and noble; which produced worthy deeds. But "the words of Jesus Christ" did far more than this: they commanded the spirit world (S. Mark i. 25); they ruled the elements (S. Matt viii. 26); they raised the dead (S. John xi. 43); they consecrated both bread and wine (S. Matt. xxvi. 26-29; xxviii. 19) and water. The power of these words is seen, moreover, in other aspects: in the love with which the poor listened to them, and "wondered at the gracious words which proceeded out of His mouth ;" in the melting of hearts which followed those blessed utterances, and which still accompanies their repetition.

IV. *Result.*—The greatness of "the words of Jesus Christ" is well seen in the results which followed upon their promulgation. They have—1) Changed the religion of the greater part of the civilized world; and they will eventually win the whole world to acknowledge their dominion. 2) Given a new life, purpose, hope, and aim to millions upon millions of immortal natures. 3) Peopled heaven with an innumerable company of the faithful; who having believed these words, have found thereby a path to heaven in the midst of the toils, cares, sins, and sorrows of this mortal life. The result of His words will only be fully known at the last day, when their greatness will be made manifest to all, both angels and men.

Epilogue.—Are these great words abiding in your souls? Do you—1) Listen to them, meditate and think them over, as guides of life? 2) Love them for the sake of Him Who spake them? 3) Obey them, remembering that a precept is attached to every promise?

SERMON XLVIII.

CONSCIENCE.

" Conscience also bearing witness."—*Rom.* ii. 15.

Origen.—" The Apostle says that they used the testimony of a good conscience who had 'the law written in their hearts.' Hence it seems necessary to inquire what that is which the Apostle calls 'conscience,' whether it be not something else beside heart or mind. This faculty is said elsewhere to 'condemn' and 'not to condemn' (1 S. John iii. 20, 21); and that it shall judge man, yet itself shall not be judged; for, 'If our heart condemn us not,' says John, 'then have we confidence towards God.' And again, Paul himself says in another place, ' Our rejoicing is this, the testimony of our conscience.' (2 Cor. i. 12.) Because I observe, therefore, that its liberty is so great that it ever rejoices and exults indeed in good deeds, but that in evil deeds it is not attacked, but it reproves and attacks the soul itself to which it adheres; I apprehend that it is the Spirit which by the Apostle is said to be with the soul as a pedagogue, and as a certain companion and ruler to it, that it may advise the soul concerning better things, or may chastise and condemn it concerning faults; about which also the Apostle says, 'What man knoweth the things of a man, save the spirit of man which is in him'? (1 Cor. ii. 11); and itself is the spirit of conscience of which he says, 'The Spirit itself beareth witness with our spirit.' (Rom. viii. 16.) And perhaps this, itself, is the Spirit who coheres with the 'souls of the righteous,' and that therefore it is written, 'O ye spirits and souls of the righteous, bless ye the Lord.' (Dan. iii. 86. Vulg.) If the soul, truly, is disobedient and contumacious to it, it will be divided and separated from it after death. And this, I think, is expressed in the Gospel concerning the unjust servant, that the Lord 'shall cut him asunder, and appoint his portion with the hypocrites.' (S. Matt. xxiv. 51.) Conscience is perhaps that spirit of which it is written, that uncorruptible 'is the spirit in man.' (Job xxxii. 8.) Which we have said before is divided and separated from the sinful soul that it may receive its portion with the hypocrites. Likewise to the soul and conscience can be adapted the expressions, 'two shall be in the field,' etc., and "two women shall be grinding at the mill.' (S. Matt. xxiv. 40, 41.)"—*In Epist. ad Rom. Geneb.* vol. ii. p. 309, D. E.

Conscience then may be defined to be the spirit which leads, plays the pedagogue to, and otherwise influences the soul. As such, conscience becomes "God's deputy," representing the mind and will of God to man. As the deputy of God, the conscience—

I. *Observes.*—Being, as it were, an eye of God. Nothing escapes God's eye, but "all things are naked and open unto the eyes of Him with Whom we have to do." (Heb. iv. 13.) Conscience observes—1) Perpetually. For "God neither slumbers nor sleeps" (Ps. cxxi. 4); and there is no intermission in the watchfulness of conscience. Whensoever the soul is capable of action, its companion, conscience, is awake to its every motion. 2) Narrowly. Being ever present with the soul, nothing can escape the searching eye of this spirit. The half-formed thought, the inclinations which have not as yet taken definite forms, are alike clear to the conscience. No concealment of any kind is possible in the smaller as well as in the greater matters. 3) Openly. The observing presence of conscience is ever felt, known, and recognized, not as a secret spy, but as an appointed observer; conscience takes note of man's every thought, word, and deed.

How careful should man become with such a sleepless, watchful, inseparable companion ever by him.

II. *Judges.*—Conscience, as God's deputy, not only observes the smallest thought, desire, and emotion of the will, as well as every word or deed, but it also passes judgment upon that which it sees. Which judgment is—1) Just. Conscience is as true as is that Master whom it represents; its judgments, therefore, must be perfectly just; they are not in any degree perverted by inclination, emotion, or any other passion; for conscience is passionless, even as God is without passions. 2) Final. Being just, there can be no appeal against the judgment of the conscience; there remains nothing in its sentence upon which an appeal could be founded. 3) Immediate. Instant judgment is passed by the conscience; almost before the thought has had time to shape itself, its approval or its disapproval has gone forth. Conscience is an immediate Court of Appeal: hence its power of checking the rising thought or wish; of staying the word as yet unspoken; of hindering the action about to be performed. 4) Inevitable. There is no escape from this tribunal of "God's deputy." Conscience speaks whether the mind will hear it or not; it will pass its decree and its judgment, even when by every device men shut their ears to, and try to stay, its "still small voice" of reproof. May you, by holy thought and action, change this judge into a friend; an accuser into a comforter.

III. *Witnesses.*—Conscience is an inward witness. "Their conscience also bearing witness." (Rom. ii. 15.) This witness, as "God's deputy"—1) Condemns every unholy and un-Christlike thought; every offence against received grace, light, knowledge, and opportunity; every unkind thought, word, or deed directed against another; everything in short, that does despite to man's better, higher, and holier nature. Worthy of all thanksgiving is such a witness as this; guarding against yielding to many a temptation; preventing the commission of many a sin. 2) Absolves; even when the doing itself may be wrong, if the intent be but good and true, let the motive be ever so misunderstood and wrongly read. There is a mighty comfort in the absolution of conscience when it is freely and entirely granted. A real confidence is begotten towards men, as well as towards God, when our heart condemns us not. (1 S. John iii. 21.) Conscience sustains under many an undeserved hardship; it cheers under many an otherwise blighting discouragement. Outward praise is valueless when it is compared with the peace of an absolving conscience.

IV. *Records.*—The recording conscience is a never-dying worm—a never-quenched fire—at the last day giving up its record before the Judgment-seat and the assembled multitudes. It records—1) During the present. After the commission of some great sin, its record becomes at length often so painful that confession of it has, of sheer necessity, to be made. The soul becomes unequal to the effort of bearing about with it the tormenting records of an avenging conscience, that is at once sleepless and unforgetful. It records also many a past conflict under temptation; many a struggle, and many a victory too. 2) At the eternal future. In heaven or hell, for ever and ever, it will deliver in its final record.

Epilogue.—How do you treat this solemn inhabitant of the soul? 1) Put it to sleep, like David (2 Sam. xii. 7); like the brethren of Joseph (Gen. xlii. 21); like Belshazzar? (Dan. v. 5.) 2) Or harden it, searing it as with a hot iron? (1 Tim. iv. 2.) Strive and pray, that "God's deputy" may be tended and preserved; exalted and made much of, as being the truest and best of all friends. Seek to gain a conscience—1) Purged from dead works. (Heb. ix. 14.) 2) Void of offence towards God and man. (Acts xxiv. 16.) 3) Witnessing in all things to that which in God's sight is true, just, and holy.

SERMON XLIX.

THE ONE GOSPEL.

"Preach the Gospel."—*S. Mark* xvi. 15.

Origen.—" *Megethius* [a Marcionite]. 'On the other hand I argue, that the Gospels are false; for the Apostle calls the Gospel one (Gal. i. 8, 9; 1 Cor. ix. 16); but you have mentioned four.'

" *Adamantius* [Orthodox]. ' The Evangelists, indeed, are four, but the Gospel one; for they have proclaimed one Christ, and enunciated the same thing. But if, therefore, each of them had proclaimed or preached another and a different Christ, you would have said rightly; but if the four speak of one Christ, the Gospels are no longer four, but one.'

" *Meg.* ' The Apostle does not say, " According to my Gospels," but " according to my Gospel." (Rom. ii. 16.) He pronounces it to be one when he says, " Though we or an angel from heaven preach any other Gospel." (Gal. i. 8.) When he says that they are one, how do you contend that they are four?'

"*Adam.* 'We say that the Gospel is one, but the Evangelists four.'"—*Cont. Marc. Sec.* i. *Wetst.* p. 9.

Our Blessed Lord does not say, "Preach the Gospels," but "Preach the Gospel;" "the Gospel," plainly implying that there are not many but one; "the" Gospel to be preached. Hence it is wrong to say, as some do, "The Gospel of SS. Matthew, Mark," etc.; it is "the Gospel"—the one Gospel, that is—"according to SS. Matthew," etc. As there is "one faith, one Lord," etc. (Eph. iv. 5), so there is one Gospel, and only one; "One Lord Jesus Christ, by Whom are all things, and we in Him." (1 Cor. viii. 6). The Gospel is one for it—

I. *Concerns one Person.*—The "one Lord Jesus Christ" is the sum and centre of the Gospel. Whatsoever additions Revelation may have made to His life, they are but expansions of that which is contained in the Gospels in the germ. The closer men adhere to the plain teaching of the Gospels, the purer, clearer, and more catholic will be their faith. The works and words of Jesus are all-sufficient for salvation. The Gospel is not so much a system of Theology—although it is that—as a personal record of personal application to the hearts and consciences of all. S. Paul elaborates the theory of Justification; Jesus Christ gives the precepts for, and the example of, a holy life, which must through Him lead on to glory and immortality. His wondrous Person in its Divine and inspired record forms the foundation and the substance of our faith. Jesus Christ was one and wholly alone in His—1) Divinity. The only Divine and sinless One Whom the world has seen or ever will see. He is God; the Maker of all things; the Opener of heaven; the Unfastener of hell; the Conqueror of death; the Ransomer from Satan; the world's God, as well as the world's Great Teacher and Prophet. 2) Humanity. Jesus Christ is the One Perfect Man; truly man, bone of our bone, flesh of our flesh; the Head of the new family of man; the Prince and Redeemer of our common humanity. "The one Gospel" is a record of the life of the "Pattern and Representative Man," of Whom the whole family in heaven and earth is named. 3) Union of the Godhead with the Manhood. Jesus was and is both God and Man. He was truly God when, as a babe, He lay in the manger in the cradle at Bethlehem; and is truly Man, now seated at God's right hand, "far above all principalities and powers;" truly Man, standing "in the midst of the elders, a Lamb as it had been slain." (Rev. v. 6.) This hypostatic union of the two natures— the Divine and the human—makes the Gospel of Jesus Christ to be "the one Gospel;" existing, distinct and alone and separate from every other message of mercy or of light which has ever fallen upon this sin-ridden world. " Preach the Gospel "—" the one Gospel "— which testifies of Me.

II. *Relates one Message.*—Which is singular, and one which men would have least expected to receive. It has several characteristics which belong to itself alone. It is—1) Sublime, yet simple. Sublime, in the promises it holds out ; in the hopes which it sets before man ; in the lofty aims and principles of action which it inculcates. Simple, in the plain and homely precepts, which all men can understand, in which its message is delivered. No mere human composition could have clothed such mighty truths in such simple language, and have so adapted them to the wants and experiences of men. 2) Saving. From many of the mistakes and pitfalls of life ; from the misdirection of many powers and the loss of opportunities in this life ; and from the greatest of all losses, that of eternal life in the world beyond the grave. 3) Adaptive. Since the precepts and promises of the Gospel come home to every emotion and temptation of the heart; to every circumstance and condition of life. Considered as a temporal message only, the lessons of the Saviour are full of wisdom ; considered as an eternal message, they are of inestimable and priceless value. They reach all the circumstances of every condition and estate of man. In this adaptive power, "the one Gospel" of Jesus

Christ stands out alone, clear and distinct from any other.

III. *Produces one Effect.*—It has changed the opinions and thoughts of the entire civilized world. There is much sin and sorrow still in the world, yet this "one Gospel" has regenerated—1) Nations. Brought them from darkness to light; redeemed them from the power of Satan unto God; altered their laws; ameliorated their condition. 2) Men. Mighty indeed is the power of this "one Gospel" upon the human heart. It has infused new life; given new hope; it has led men from a sad and ruined estate to recover their lost birthright as sons of that God by Whom they themselves and the world were made. 3) Creation. For it will deliver "the creature itself from the bondage of corruption," and vindicate at the last God's final purpose in the creation of the world and of man. Judged by its mere effect alone, the Gospel of Jesus stands out in the world's history as one grand exception in the world, and as a heaven-sent means for the regeneration and purification of a lost and fallen race. It is essentially "one Gospel" in result.

IV. *Tends to one Issue.*—For this "one Gospel" is one in substance. There is an intrinsic harmony— 1) In every part of this Gospel. No contradiction can be found in it. One part of it agrees with the other entirely and perfectly. It forms one harmonious and perfect whole. 2) In the means which it proposes for the instauration of man's estate. On God's part, "acceptance through the Beloved;" on man's part, obedience to and conformity with the mind and will of Jesus Christ. 3) In the end and issue of its working, which tends to the relief of man's condition here, and to his final salvation hereafter, and to the glory of God. Nothing is opposed to this one message of glad tidings; which rejoices alike the heart of man and the highest heavens. Preach the Gospel—this "one Gospel"—which is a consistent and harmonious body of Divine truth.

Epilogue.—This "one Gospel" is the heritage of the faithful, as being the great tradition of that Church which is the Body of Christ. Let each member of the Church ask his heart, Is it my Gospel? Do I love it? Do I obey it? Live for it, and hope to die in it?

SERMON L.

NIGHT.

"It was night."—*S. John* xiii. 30.

Origen.—" This sensible night one must read as an image of the night that was in the soul when 'darkness was upon the face of the deep' (Gen. i. 2); for 'Satan entered into Him.' (S. John xiii. 27.) 'The darkness He called night.' (Gen. i. 5.) Wherefore Paul says we are not children of the night; declaring, 'We are not of the night nor of the darkness.' (1 Thess. v. 5.) Again, 'Let us who are of the day be sober.' (1 Thess. v. 8.) Wherefore it was not night to those whose feet were washed by Jesus, but it was the most splendid day to those who, being cleansed, had cast off the defilements in the feet of their souls; and especially it was not night to him who 'was leaning on Jesus' bosom' (S. John xiii. 23); because Jesus loved him, and by that love cast out all the darkness."—*Comment in Joan. Huet.* vol. ii. p. 412, A. B.

The physical darkness which reigned at the time of the natural night when Judas the traitor went out from the Presence of the Lord, was typical of the far denser and more terrible spiritual darkness of soul which falls upon those who go out in spirit from the Presence of the Lord, casting away all their faith, love, and obedience to Him. Night is often in Holy Scripture used as an emblem of sin; but it is also in itself a type, both clear and expressive, of the effects of sin. As light is the fitting emblem of purity, hope, usefulness, and knowledge, so darkness is a most apt similitude of sin, despair, vanity, and ignorance. Our Blessed Lord was "The True Light, which lighteth every man that cometh into the world." (S. John i. 9.) Satan is "the power of darkness." (Col. i. 13.) Rightly then is it said that at this time, when "it was night," immediately before Judas "went out," "Satan entered into him." (S. John xiii. 27.) Tracing some few analogies between the natural night of the day and the spiritual night of the soul, we note that these nights are alike—

I. *Terrible.*—The ninth plague—that of darkness— lasted for only three days, yet it affected the Egyptians more than any of those which had gone before. Darkness is—1) Terrible, as awakening fear. It gives rise to many an unreal suspicion and imagination. In the darkness, when moved by fear, man sees danger everywhere. The night of sin ever brings fear and suspicion in its train, judging all things by its imperfect and unholy standard. The shadows and fancies of a darkened soul, though unreal, are more terrible to bear than are the saddest experiences of actual life. 2) Terrible, as confining the soul in the house of wickedness. "Neither rose any from his place for three days." (Exod. x. 23.) Whilst the night lasts there is no going forth, no progress, no change; the soul is shut up in its own place, devoid alike of help and hope. When the soul goes out of its own house to Jesus Christ, there comes light, and joy, and peace to it; out of its own house, to commune with the good and the wise, then also are all the mists and obscurities of night cleared away. Without escape from the house of darkness there can be no real improvement or lasting deliverance. 3) Terrible, as depressing the soul. Paralyzing all its healthy action; generating therein many a morbid growth; so weakening it as to render it unfitted to bear any very bright manifestation of the Sun of Righteousness and of truth. Terrible, indeed, was that night of the soul in which Judas, possessed by Satan, "went out" to the betrayal of his Lord.

II.—*Dangerous.*—Night brings a certain amount of danger with it. In the night a man cannot discern —1) Secret enemies. They may be "about his path and spying out all his ways," yet he cannot see them; lurking hither, and lying thither, in this or that dark nook or corner. Hence he is easily attacked, and still more easily overcome; for, although suspicious, he is usually unprepared. It is so also with the soul that walks "on in darkness;" it is unconscious of the whereabouts of its spiritual enemies, which are lurking in ambush, waiting for it on every side; it is easily attacked, since it knows not which is the proper side to guard, which temptation will attack it with the direst force; and it is, alas, but too easily overcome, since its weapons of defence are not ready for use, and its arm has lost much of its old power to defend and to strike. 2) Hidden dangers. There is no long highway in the world that is absolutely free from danger if trodden in darkness. The way of life is more dangerous to traverse than any earthly way or road: it is subject to more dangerous pitfalls; it is beset with severer stumblingblocks. 3) The right way. In the night the traveller cannot see the path before him; he is liable to "wander out of the way," nay, to so alter his course, that he may be going backwards instead of forwards. When the night of the soul is very dark, it cannot find out the "way of holiness;" the "way of peace." It walks on still in darkness, with all its foundations put out of course.

III. *Unprofitable.*—" The night cometh when no man can work" (S. John ix. 4), "work" that is to any advantage or profit. In total darkness there is total idleness; but the dusky light of night allows certain works to be done which are called "the unfruitful works of darkness." (Eph. v. 11.) The night of the soul is therefore unprofitable—1) In thought. What brightness and purity of thought can arise in a benighted soul? How dim must be its eye of faith; how limited its conceptions; how dull and "slow of heart" to enter into the thoughts of those who rejoice in the light of the true, the beautiful, and the good. 2) In word. "Out of the abundance of the heart the mouth speaketh;" as the thought is, so is the speech; where the one is profitless, the other must be of little or no value. 3) In deed. For action, like speech, is also the product of thought. It is motive which both originates and ennobles or debases action. The enlightened act with enlightenment; the benighted and ignorant are equally consistent in their deeds. When the "Light of the World" shined upon the souls of men, it was to give them "light in the Lord," that all the unprofitableness might be taken from them; that their lives might be redeemed from destruction, and crowned with lovingkindness and tender mercy.

IV. *Solitary.*—During their three days and three

nights of darkness, the Egyptians "saw not one another." They were deprived of all external association; each one remained solitary and alone. The night of the soul is likewise solitary; for sin by its darkness separates it from—1) God, Who is light. For "what communion hath light with darkness?" (2 Cor. vi. 14); which separation becomes to it an eternal and an irreparable loss. 2) Good men. From "the children of light;" cutting the soul off wholly from "the communion of Saints;" from having any "part or lot" in their matters, life, aims, objects, or estate. 3) "One another." Since darkness engenders suspicion, distrust, and fear, between those who are dwelling in the same region of darkness. Judas "went out" alone; he suffered his remorse alone; he died alone, an outcast from his fellows; separated from all his kind, the night of his soul and body was solitary indeed.

Epilogue.—Like the Beloved Disciple, may you come to Jesus Christ the "True Light," and He will make "all your darkness," and sin, and doubt of soul "to be light." He will fill you with the light of—1) Love; which forms the brightness of the Cherubim. 2) Truth; so that you can never err and fall away from grace. 3) Holiness; clothing you with a heavenly and a Divine light, as with the garment of the Lord; the vestments fit and proper for the children of the day. "For days are understood to be the precepts and dogmas of truth, placed in the Scriptures for the illumination of intelligent souls."—*Origen in Matt. Tract* xxix. *Geneb.* ii. p. 92, G.

www.ingramcontent.com/pod-product-compliance
Lightning Source LLC
Chambersburg PA
CBHW032055220426
43664CB00008B/1012